Josiah Child, Thomas Culpeper

A New Discourse of Trade

Wherein are recommended several weighty points, relating to companies of merchants. The act of navigation. Naturalization of strangers, and our woollen manufactures

Josiah Child, Thomas Culpeper

A New Discourse of Trade
Wherein are recommended several weighty points, relating to companies of merchants. The act of navigation. Naturalization of strangers, and our woollen manufactures

ISBN/EAN: 9783337348090

Printed in Europe, USA, Canada, Australia, Japan

A New
DISCOURSE
OF
TRADE,

Wherein is Recommended ſeveral weighty Points relating to Companies of **Merchants**.

The Act of NAVIGATION.

NATURALIZATION of Srangers.

And our **Woolen Manufactures**.

The

BALLANCE of TRADE.

And the Nature of Plantations, and their Conſequences in Relation to the Kingdom, are ſeriouſly Diſcuſſed.

Methods for the Employment and Maintenance of the Poor are Propoſed.

The Reduction of Intereſt of Money to 4 *l. per Centum*, is Recommended.

And ſome Propoſals for erecting a Court of Merchants for determining Controverſies, relating to Maritine Affairs, and for a Law for Transferrance of Bills of Debts, are humbly Offered.

By Sir Joſiah Child.

London, Printed and Sold by *T. Sowle*, next Door to the *Meeting-houſe* in *White-Hart-Court* in *Gracious-ſtreet*, and at the *Bible* in *Leaden-hall-ſtreet*, near the Market, 1698.

December 24. 1692.

IMPRIMATUR

Edmund Bohun.

THE PREFACE.

THE following *Answer* to that Treatise, Entituled, *Interest of Money mistaken*, I wrote long before the last Session of Parliament, that began the 19th of *October* 1669. but fore-seeing that that Session might be engaged in greater Debates of another Nature, and in consequence not have leisure to consider this Subject, I deferred the Printing of it, since which I have seen another Treatise, wrote by *Thomas Manly*, Gentleman, endeavouring to prove, That it will be for the Advantage of this Kingdom, to continue the Interest of *Money* at 6 *per Cent*, but after several Perusals of his Treatise, I must needs say, that either I understand nothing of this subject, or else this Gentleman is the greatest Stranger to it that ever undertook to Discourse it, he having writ much, but in my Opinion nothing to the purpose, more than was much better (though briefliер) said by the Author of the fore-mentioned Treatise, out of which most of his seems to be borrowed, though the Words be varied, with some additions of Interrogations, Expostulations, Similies and Circumlocutions.

Besides, the Gentleman taking up things at random, and for want of a due understanding of the Matter, is very unfortunate in his Instances of *Fact, viz.*

In his Preface, about the middle, his Words are, *Has Abatement of Usury, or some other sublime Policy, obliged the* French *of late to set upon Trade and Manufactures?* And then he affirms, that I dare not touch on that String, in regard that Nation hath not for many Years altered Interest from 7 *per Cent.*

To his Interrogation I answer positively, That the Abatement of Usury hath done it; and if you will not believe

lieve me, read the *French* Edicts themselves, and they will tell you so; an Abstract of one whereof I have recited in the following Treatise.

To his Affirmation, that I dare not touch upon this String; I say, I dare do it, and put the whole issue upon this, for the *French* in Fact have brought down the Use of Money under 6 *per Cent*, and that to 5 *per Cent* lately; as I have been credibly informed, and do believe; and if they had omitted this, all their buslings in other things would signifie *very little* in *Conclusion*.

The *Sweeds* likewise since they Established their *Council of Trade*, and set themselves to the consideration of making themselves consierable by Trade, have reduced their Interest from 10 to 6 *per Cent*.

His following Words are, *Do* Italy *and* Holland *owe their Trade and Riches to the lowness of Usury, or to their innate Frugality, wonderful Industry, and admirable Arts*, &c.

I answer, *Low Interest* is the Natural

Mother of Frugality Induſtry and Arts, which I hope the *Gentleman*'s Eyes will be open enough to ſee by that time he hath read a little further, and conſidered two or three Years longer.

But it may be ſaid, How can a low Intereſt be the natural Mother of Frugality, when if this Gentleman be to be believed, *Abatement of our Uſe-Money brought in our Drinking*: Which he does not only ſay, but prove as he thinks by an inſtance of Fact; for he ſays, we now ſpend uſually twenty Thouſand Tuns of *French* Wine, (and he believes that a far greater quantity is yearly Imported) and that the Computation of *Spaniſh*, *Rheniſh* and *Levant* Wines far exceeds the former, ſo that by his calculate, and as he ſays, grounded upon a very good Authority, *viz.* a *Report* to the Houſe of *Commons*, it ſhould ſeem that there is about the Quantity of forty five Thouſand Tuns of Wine of all ſorts Imported annually into *England*.

But if it ſhall appear in Fact that before the laſt abatement of Intereſt from

8 to 6 *per Cent*, we did uſually import near twice the Quantity of Wines annually we now do, and that now in all ſorts of Wines we do not Import above the quantity of twenty thouſand Tuns yearly; then what will become of his large Structure, built upon a Sandy Foundation?

Reader, this is the Caſe, and the matter of Fact truly recited by me, (which many of the Honourable *Members* of the Houſe of *Commons* well know) and miſtaken by him; from whence I might with much more reaſon infer, that the Abatement of Intereſt drove out our *Drinking* (ſo *pro tanto* it did) but I know there were likewiſe other Cauſes for it, eſpecially the Additional Duties, that from time to time have been laid upon Wines.

But before I part with the *Gentleman* on this point, I muſt note to him another Monſtrous miſtake in Fact, or at leaſt in his Inference, *viz.* he ſays, that twenty thouſand Tuns of *French* Wines at 2 *Shil.* 8 *pence per* Gallon amounts to

640000

640000 *l.* and concludes (if I understand him) that so much is lost to *England*; whereas, were the Matter of Fact as he supposeth, which it is not so in any measure, this inference would be strangly erroneous; for by the expence of such quantity we can rationally loose only the first cost, which is but about 6 or 7 *Pound per* Tun, and that amounts to but 120000 *l.* or 140000 *l.* at the utmost all the rest being *Freight*, *Custom*, and *Charges* paid to the *King*, and our own Country-men, and consequently not lost to *England*.

To conclude this *Head*, I do agree fully with the *Gentleman*, that *Luxury* and *Prodigality* are as well prejudicial to *Kingdoms* as to Private *Families*; and that the expence of Foreign Commodities, especially foreign Manufactures, is the worst expence a Nation can be inclinable to, and ought to be prevented as much as possible, but that nothing hath or will incline this or any other Nation more to Thriftiness and good Husbandry, than Abatement of Interest, I think

think I have proved in the following Diſcourſe, and that therefore all that this Gentleman hath ſaid about Luxury, *&c.* is againſt himſelf, and for leſſening of Intereſt.

The *Gentleman* at the beginning of his Preface ſaith, *He will not inquire into the lawfulneſs of Intereſt, but leave the ſcrupulous to the ſeveral Diſcourſes made publick on that ſubject.* For my part I ſhall agree with him in that likewiſe; and to the intent that what hath been made publick formerly may the better be known, I would intreat thoſe that would be throughly ſatisfied therein, diligently to peruſe an excellent Treatiſe Entituled, *The Engliſh Uſur, or Uſury condemned, being a Collection of the Opinions of many of the Learned Fathers of the Church of* England, *and other Divines,* Printed at *London, Anno* 1634, and now about to be reprinted.

But upon this occaſion I ſhall humbly preſume to ſay, that if by the following Diſcourſes it ſhall appear, that the Intereſt of *England* being higher then

that

that of our Neighbour Country, it doth render our Lands (our common Mother) of vile and base esteem; doth prevent the cultivation and improvement of our Country, as otherwise it might and would be improved; doth hinder the growth of Trade and imployment and increase of the Hands of our Country; doth eucourage Idleness and Luxury, and discourage Navigation, Industry, Arts and Invention; then I make no question, but the taking of such an *Interest* as exceeds the Measure of our Neighbours, is **Malum in se**, by the light of Nature, and consequently a Sin, although God had never expresly forbid it.

But the *Usurer* may say, suppose the *Borrower* makes 12 *per cent* of my Money, is it a Sin in me to take 6 *per cent* of him? I answer, between them two there may be no commutative Injustice, according to my weak Judgment, while each retains a mutual Benefit, the *Usurer* for his Money, the *Borrower* for his Industry; but in the mean time if the

the Rate given and taken exceed the Rate of our Neighbour Nations, these fatal National Evil Consequences will ensue to our common Country by such a Practice, which therefore I conclude to be **Malum in se**: And peradventure therefore the Wisdom of God Almighty did prohibite the *Jews* from lending upon Use one to another, but allowed them to lend to Strangers for the Enriching of their own Nation, and Improvement of their own Teritory, and for the Impoverishing of others, those to whom they were permitted to lend, being such only whom they were commanded to destroy, or at least to keep Poor and Miserable, as the *Gibeonites*, *&c.* Hewers of Wood, and Drawers of Water.

I purpose to do the Gentleman that right as not to omit taking notice of any thing he hath of novelty in relation to the present Controversie, whether it be material or no; and in order thereunto, the next thing I observe new in his Treatise, is, Pag. 9. it is, saith he, *Dear-*

Dearneſs of Wages that ſpoils the Engliſh *Trade, and abaſes our Lands, not Uſury*; and therefore he propounds the making a Law to retrench the Hire of *Poor Mens* Labour (*an honeſt charitable Project, and well becoming a* Uſurer) the Anſwer to this is eaſie.

1*ſt*, I affirm, and can prove he is miſtaken in fact, for the *Dutch* with whom we principally contend in Trade, give generally more Wages to all their *Manufacturers* by at leaſt two pence in the Shilling, than the *Engliſh*.

2*dly*, Where ever Wages are high univerſally throughout the whole *World*, it is an infallible evideuce of the Riches of that Country: And where-ever Wages for Labour runs low, it is a proof of the Poverty of that place.

3*dly*, It is multitudes of People, and good Laws, ſuch as cauſe an encreaſe of People, which principally Enrich any Country; and if we retrench by Law the Labour of our People, we drive them from us to other Countries that give better Rates, and ſo the

Dutch

Dutch have drained us of our *Sea-men* and *Woollen Manufactures*; and *We*, the *French* of their *Artificers* and *Silk-Manufacturers*, and of many more we ſhould if our Laws otherwiſe gave them fitting Encouragement, whereof more in due place.

4*thly*, If any particular Trades exact more here than in *Holland*, they are only ſuch as do it by vertue of Incorporations, Priviledges and Charters, whereof the Cure is eaſie by an Act of *Naturalization*, and without Compulſitory Laws.

It is true, our great Great-*Grand-Fathers* did exerciſe ſuch a Policy of endeavouring to retrench of the Price of Labour by a Law (altho' they could never effect it) but that was before *Trade* was introduced into this *Kingdom*; we are ſince, with the reſt of the Trading World, grown wiſer in this Matter, and I hope ſhall ſo continue.

The next new Objection the *Gentleman* hath is Page. 13. *If we abate Intereſt* (ſaid he) *will not the* Hollander *take the*

ſame

same course, while we, like Children, Wink, and think no body sees us.

Yes, certainly the *Dutch* will take the same course, except they leave their old wont, for we never yet Abated our Interest, but they soon Abated theirs; but what if they do? We having brought our Interest to 4 *per cent*, shall have them against a Wall, we know the length of their Tedder, they cannot run much farther from us, so that if we Wink, it is not like Children, as the Gentleman supposeth, but if we take his Advice, we shall Wink like *Children*, while other *Nations* strike us by Abating their Interest.

2. If we cannot gain all we would of them presently, we shall gain the more from other parts of the World, that cannot suddenly Abate their Interest to any Proportion with ours.

3. Why shall we absolutely conclude that other Nations will do it? May we not think that some Parts or People in the World, may be as un-fore-seeing as this Gentleman pretends to be, and not know

know it is for their Advantage to lower their Intereſt, though we know it to be ours?

4. Why may we not think that Corruption, Avarice and *Uſurers*, may be ſo prevalent in ſome Parts of the *World*, or to obſtruct ſo Good and National a Work as this?

I omit ſeveral other Errors in Fact that the Gentleman is guilty of in the courſe of his Writing, and muſt needs be ſo, having taken up his Notions (for want of Experience) upon truſt from others, who perhaps underſtand as little as himſelf, *viz.* Page 16. he ſaith, *Our vent into* Spain *and* Portugal *is greatly leſſened*, and conſequently he reckons them two Trades, among others loſt in whole or in part; ſo great a miſtake, that I dare affirm, and appeal to the Record of the *Cuſtom-Houſe* Books, for a Judgment in this Caſe, that thoſe two Trades, as to our native Exportations, are more than treebled within leſs than 30 Years.

Page 21. he ſaith, that, *If Wages*, &c.

were

were as cheap, and Usury as low with us as in Holland, *yet if our* Merchants *live at so great a rate as now they do, how is it possible we should thrive on as easie Gains as those who spend so much less, and Trade so much more?*

I answer, There is nothing in the World will engage our *Merchants* to Spend less and Trade more, than the Abatement of Interest, for the subduing of Interest will bring in multitudes of Traders, as it hath in *Holland*, to such a degree that almost all their People of both Sexes are Traders, and the many Traders will necessitate *Merchants* to Trade for less Profit, and consequently be more frugal in their Expences, which is the true Reason why many considerable *Merchants* are against the lessening of *Interest*, whereof I have said some-whet more in the following Treatis.

Page 43. He Propounds another remedy for the advance of our Trade, and the keeping our Coin at home, and enlargeth much upon it in his Appendix, which

which is *to diminish the intrinsick value of our Coin*.

If the *Gentleman* had understood *Trade* half so well, as he is said to do *Mortgages*, *Bonds* and *Bills*, certainly he would not have mentioned this old threed-bare and exploded Project, which is a trick hath been tried so often in *Spain*, till it hath left them more black Money (as they call it) than white or yellow, notwithstanding their Silver Mines in *Peru* and *Mexico*, and that their Laws make it Death to export Gold or Silver.

This Conceit I have known three times experienced likewise in *Portugal*, with in this 24 or 25 years, at first the piece of 8 Rials went at 400 Ries; after that was brought to 480, after that to 520, and now to 600 Ries, and yet still we bring their Money from them as heretofore, and sell our commodities to them for as much Silver as ever.

The reason is evident; suppose for example, a Hat that was usually sold to them for 4 pieces of 8, when the piece of 8 was at 400 Ries, we then ſold ſuch a Hat for 1600 Ries; when they raiſed the piece of eight 80 Ries *per* piece more, we ſold the ſame Hat at 2000 Ries, and ſo riſing in propotion as they raiſed their Coin; the *Merchant* ſtill obſerving what the intrinſick value of the Money is, not the name it is called by, and ſo it would be in *England*, or any part of the World.

I have now done with all I can find of novelty in this Gentlemans Treatiſe; to meddle with old and ſtale matter, which in other words hath been often ſaid, and as often anſwered, would be but to trouble the *Reader* with Impertinencies; ſo would it likewiſe to uſe opprobrious, calumniating Reflections, as he doth covertly in a buſineſs of that ſeriouſneſs, weight and publick concernment as this is; I underſtand not the World ſo little as not to know, that he that will faithfully ſerve his Country, muſt be content to paſs through good Report and evil Report, neither regard I which I meet with, **Truth I am ſure**

at

at last will vindicate it self, and be found by my Country-men.

Yet before I conclude this *Preface*, I must needs take notice of one thing to be wondred at, *viz.* That some had the Confidence publickly to assert before the *Lords*, when this Controversie was debated before their *Lordships*; that when Interest was at 10 *per cent*, Land was sold at 20 years Purchase; a strange, presumptuous and incredible Assertion against Records, against Experience, and against Reason; to which I doubt not but their *Lordships* will be able to give a full confutation out of their own Memorials, before this be made publick.

And for the Reason of it, will any Man believe that our Fathers were so stupid, as to lay out their Money in Land not to see it again in twenty Years, when at single Interest at ten *per cent* they might double their Money in 10 years, at Interest upon Interest in seven years?

I have been told by a person of very

great Honour, that this *Gentleman* himſelf, in his private diſcourſe, confeſſeth, that the Abatement of Intereſt will advance the value of Land, but he queſtion's whether it will encreaſe Trade; certainly a needleſs ſcruple to any Man, that ſhall deliberately conſider the inſeparable affinity that is in all Nations, and at all times, between Land and Trade, which are Twins, and have always, and ever will wax and wane together, *It cannot be ill with Trade but Land will fall, nor ill with Lands but Trade will feel it.*

But in regard, this *Gentleman* is ſo miſerably miſtaken in the Trade of *Spain* and *Potugal*, which he reckons as loſt, I think it may be uſeful to inform him and others better, what Trades are really loſt; and enquire how we came to looſe them? And what Trades we ſtill retain, and why? And of both as briefly as I can; becauſe I have ſaid ſome thing of them in the following Treatiſe.

Of

Of Trades Loſt.

1. The *Ruſſia* Trade, where the *Dutch* had laſt year 22 Sail of great Ships, and the *Engliſh* but one, whereas formerly we had more of that Trade than the *Dutch*.

2. The *Green-land* Trade where the *Dutch* and *Hamburgers* have yearly at leaſt 4 or 500 Sail of Ships, and the *Engliſh* but one laſt year, and none the former.

3. The great Trade of *Salt* from St. *Vuals* in *Portugal* and from *France*, with *Salt*, *Wine* and *Brandy* to the *Eaſt-lands*.

4. All that vaſt and notorious *Trade of Fiſhing for White-Herrings*, upon our own Coaſt.

5. The *Eaſt-Country* Trade, in which we have not half ſo much to do as we had formerly, and the *Dutch* ten times more than they had in times paſt.

6. A very great part of our *Trade for Spaniſh-Woolls* from *Bilvao*. Theſe Trades and ſome more I could name, the *Dutch* Intereſt of 3 *per cent*, and nar-

row limited Companies in *England* have beat us out of.

7. The *East-India Trade* for *Nutmegs Cloves* and *Mace* (an extraordinary profitable Trade) the *Dutch* Arms and Sleights have beat us out of; but their lower Interest gave strength to their Arms, and acuteness to their Invention.

8. Their great *Trade for China* and *Japan* (whereof we have no share) is an effect of their low Interest, these Trades not being to be obtained but by a long process, and great disbursements, destitute of present, but with expectation of future Gain, which *6 per cent* cannot bear.

9. The Trade of *Scotland* and *Ireland*, two of our own Kingdoms, the *Dutch* have bereaved us of, and in effect wholly engrossed to themselves; which their low Interest hath been the principal engine, though I know other accidents have contributed thereunto, whereof more hereafter.

10. The *Trade for Norway* is in great part

part lost to the *Danes*, *Holsteners*, &c. by reason of some clauses in the *Act* of *Navigation*, whereof more in due place.

11. A very great part of the *French Trade* for Exportation is lost, by reason of great *Impositions* laid there upon our *Draperies*.

12. A great part of the *Plate Trade* from *Cadiz* is lost to the *Dutch*, who by reason of the lowness of their Interest, can afford to let their Stocks lie beforehand at *Seville* and *Cadiz*, against the arrival of the *Spanish Flota*, who sometimes are expected 3, 6, 9, and 12 Months before they come, especially since the late Interruptions that our *Jamaica Capers* have given them; by which means they engross the greatest part of the Silver, whereas we, in regard our Stocks run at higher Interest, cannot so well afford to keep them so long dead. It is true, the *English* have yet a share in this Trade, by reason of some after recited natural advantages, *viz. Woolen Manufactures*, *Tin*, *Lead*, *Fish*, &c. inseparably annexed by *God's* Providence to

this *Kingdom.* It is true likewise, that the *Peace* at *Munster* hath much furthered the *Dutch* in that affair; but as true it is, that their lower Interest hath enabled them to make a much greater improvement and advantage in Trade by that Peace, than ever they could otherways have done.

13. The Trade of *Surrenham*, since the *Dutch* got possession of that Country in the late War, is so totally lost to the *English*, that we have now no more Commerce with that Country, than we should have if it were sunk in the Sea; so severe and exact are the *Hollanders*, in keeping the Trades of their own Plantations intirely to their own People.

14. The Trade of *Menades* or *New-York*, we should have gained instead of the former, since we got possession of that place in the late War, if the *Dutch* had not been *connived* at therein at first, which now I hope they are not; for if they should be, it would not only be to the intire loss of that Trade to *England*,

but

but greatly to the prejudice of the *English* Trade to *Virginia*, becauſe the *Dutch*, under pretence of Trading to and from *New-York*, carry great quantites of *Virginia Tobacco* directly for *Holland*.

15. The *English Trade to Guiny* I fear is much declined, by reaſon that Company have met with Diſcouragements from ſome of our Neighbours.

Note, That moſt of the aforementioned Trades are the greateſt Trades in the World, for the employment of Shipping and Sea-men.

2dly, That no Trades deſerve ſo much care to procure, and preſerve, and encouragement to proſecute, as thoſe that employ the moſt Shipping, altho' the Commodities tranſported be of ſmall Value in themſelves; For, *Firſt*, they are certainly the moſt profitable; for beſides the gain accrewing by the Goods, the Freights, which is in ſuch Trades often more than the Value of the Goods, is all profit to the Nation; beſides, they bring with them a great

acceſs

accefs of *Power* (Hands as well as Money) *many Ships and Sea-men being juftly the reputed Strength and Safety of* England.

I could mention more Trades that we have loft, and are in the High-way to loofe, but I fhall forbear at prefent, for fear this Porch fhould prove too big; as alfo for other reafons.

The Trades we yet retain are;

1*ft*, For Fifh, The *Trade of Red-Herrings from* Yarmouth, *Pilchards in the* Weft-Country, *and Cod-fifh in* New-found-Land *and* New-England.

2*dly*, A good part of the *Turkey*, *Italian*, *Spanifh* and *Portugal* Trades.

Our Trades to and from our own *Plantations*, viz. *Virginia*, *Barbadoes*, *New-England*, *Jamaica*, and the Leward Iflands.

If any fhall here ask me, how it comes to pafs that the *Dutch* low Intereft hath not Cafhiered us of thefe *Trades*, as well as the former? I fhall anfwer, firft Generally, and then Particularly.

1. Generally, I fay, the *Dutch low*

Intereft

Interest hath miserably lessened us in all Trades of the World, not secured to us by Laws, or by some natural advantage which over-ballanceth the disproportion of our Interest of Money, which disproportion I take to be 3 *per cent.*

2. Particularly, The *Red-Herring Trade* we retain, by reason of two natural Advantages; one is, the Fish for that purpose must be brought fresh on Shore, and that the *Dutch* cannot do with theirs, because the *Herrings* swim on our Coast, and consequently at too great a distance from theirs.

The other is, those *Herrings* must be smoaked with Wood, which cannot be done on any reasonable terms, but in a Woody *Country*, such as *England* is, and *Holland* is not. These advantages that God hath given our Land do Counterpoize and Overpoize the Disproportion of Interest, viz. 3 *per cent*, otherwise we might say, Farewel *Red-Herrings*, as well as *White*.

The *Pilchards* on the West-Coast likewise come to our Shores, and must

be

be cured and pressed upon the Land, which is impossible for the *Dutch* to do.

The *New-found-Land Fishing* is managed by West-Country-Men, whose Ports are properly Scituated for that Country, *and the Country it self is his Majesties* ; *so the* Dutch *can have no footing there* ; *if they could*, 3 per cent *would soon send us home to keep Sheep.*

As to the *Turkey*, *Italian*, *Spanish* and *Portugal Trades*, though our vent for fine Cloath, and some sorts of Stuffs be declined, yet we retain a very considerable part of those Trades, by reason of some Natural, and some Artificial or Legal Advantages, which preponderates 3 *per cent* ; such as these:

1*st*, The *Wool*, of which our midling and course Cloaths are made of, is our own, and consequently cheaper to us than the *Dutch* can steal it from us, paying *Freights*, *Commission*, *Bribes* and *Cousenage*, and sometime armed *Guards* to force it off.

2*dly*, Our *Fewel* and *Victuals* is *cheaper* in remote parts from *London*, and consequently

quently our *Manufactures* can and do work cheaper than the *Dutch*, whatever Mr. *Manley* erroneously affirms.

3dly, The *Red-Herring*, *Pilchard*, *New-found-land* and *New-England Fishery*, by which we carry on much of these Trades, are inseparably annexed to this Kingdom, as before is demonstrated, and by the Bounty of *God* Almighty, not by our own Wisdom or Industry.

4thly, Our *Lead* and *Tin*, by which we carry on much of those Trades, are Natives with us.

5thly, Our *Country* consumes within it self more of *Spanish Wine and Fruit*, Zant *Currans and* Levant *Oyls*, than any Country in *Europe*.

6thly, Which is an Artificial advantage (and due to the Wisdom of the Contrivers) our *Act of Navigation* compels us, or at least would do, if it were justly administred, to import none of those Goods but from the proper Ports of their Imbarkation, and by *English* Shipping only.

The *Trades* to and from all our own

Plan-

Plantations, are likewiſe ſecured to us by the *Act of Navigation*, or would be, if that Act were truly executed, and if it were not for that, you ſhould ſee forty *Dutch* Ships at our own *Plantations* for one *Engliſh*.

To conclude this Paragraph, the *Dutch low Intereſt, through our own ſupineſs, hath robbed us totally of all Trade, not inſeparably annexed to this Kingdom by the benevolence of Divine Providence, and our Act of Navigation*; which, though it have ſome things in it wanting amendment, deſerves to be called our (**Charta Maritima**) inſomuch as, with ſhame to our ſelves, it may be truly ſaid of us, as we Proverbially ſay to careleſs Perſons, *They have loſt all that is looſe*.

When I think of theſe things, I cannot but wonder that there ſhould be found *Engliſh-men* who want not Bread to eat, or Cloaths to wear, ſhould be yet ſo unkind and hard hearted to their Country, as ſtrenuouſly to endeavour (for private Ends) the depriving her of

ſo

ſo great a good, as would be the abatement of our Intereſt to 4 *per cent*, by a Law. I have lately ſeen a Treatiſe writ about thirty Years ſince, by *Lewis Roberts*, *Merchant*, wherein he highly Exaggerates (and with great Reaſon) the wonderful advantage the *Dutch* have by the lowneſs of their *Cuſtoms*; but ſeeing an exact imitation in that reſpect is not conſiſtent with our Affairs at preſent, tho' much to be deſired in due time, I inſiſt not thereupon, but think it neceſſary by the way to make this true Animadverſion, *viz.* That 2 *per cent*, *extraordinary in Intereſt is worſe than* 4 per cent *extraordinary in Cuſtoms*; becauſe *Cuſtoms* run only upon our Goods imported or exported, and that but once for all; whereas Intereſt runs as well upon our Ships, as Goods, and muſt be yearly paid on both, ſo long as they are in being; and the Ships in many bulkey *Trades*, and ſuch as are Nationally moſt Profitable, are of four times the value of the Goods.

That old Objection about *Widows* and

Orphans,

Orphans; I have, I think, fully anſwered in my former Treatiſe; but becauſe I yet ſometimes meet with it, I ſhall ſay a word more to it here, *viz.*

1. *Widows and Orphans are not one to twenty of the whole People; and it's the Wiſdom of Law-makers to provide for the good of the Majority of People, though a Minor part ſhould a little ſuffer.*

2. *Of Widows and Orphans, not one in forty will ſuffer by the Abatement of Intereſt*, for theſe Reaſons, *viz.*

1*ſt*, Of *Widows* and *Orphans*, nine of ten in this Kingdom have very little or nothing at all left them by their Deceaſed Relations, and all ſuch will have an advantage by the Abatement of Intereſt, becauſe ſuch Abatement will encreaſe *Trade*, and in conſequence occaſion more Employment for ſuch neceſſitous Perſons.

2*dly*, Many *Widows and Orphans* have *Joyntures, Annuities, Coppyholds, and other Lands* left them, as well as Money; and all ſuch will be Gainers by the Abatement of Intereſt.

3*dly*,

3dly, For all *London Orphans* the *City* gives not now above 5, and to ſome 4 *per Cent* Intereſt, ſo the loſs to ſuch is not worth ſpeaking of.

4thly, Many *Executors* are ſo unworthy as to allow *Orphans* no Intereſt, and yet juſtifie themſelves by Law; to ſuch *Orphans* it will be all one what the legal Rate of Intereſt be.

5thly, When the Law for Abatement of *Intereſt* is paſt, many more Parents will leave their Children Annuities and Eſtates running in *Trade*, as they do in *Holland* and *Italy*, whereby the Abatement of *Intereſt* will become Profitable, not Prejudicial, to them.

And for the few that at firſt may happen to ſuffer, whereof the number will be very ſmall (and therefore not to be named in Competition with the common Good of the Kingdom) they have an eaſie means within their own Power to prevent their being one Farthing the worſe for the Abatement of *Intereſt*; it is but wearing a Lawn-Whisk inſtead of a *Point de Venice*; and for the meaner ſort, a Searge Petty-Coat, inſtead of a Silk one, and a plain pair of Shoes inſtead of Laced ones. And that the Ladies may not be offended with me, I dare undertake that this will never ſpoil but mend their *Marriages*; beſides the greater good it will bring to their Country, and to their Poſterities after them, whether they prove to be Noblemen, Gentlemen or Merchants, *&c.*

I have in ſeveral places of my enſuing Treatiſe, referred to ſome Tracts I formerly Publiſhed upon this ſubject, which, being now wholly out of Print, I thought fit to Re-print and annex unto this, which at firſt I intended not.

Some there are who would grant that *Abatement of Intereſt*, if it could be effected, would procure to the Nation all the good that I alledge it will bring with it, but ſay it is *not practicable, or at leaſt not now.*

1. A needleſs Scruple, and contradictory to Experience; for firſt, *a Law hath abated Intereſt in* England, *three times within theſe few Years already*; *and*

what ſhould hinder its effect more now than formerly?

2. If a Law will not do it, why do the *Uſurers* raiſe ſuch a duſt, and engage ſo many Friends to oppoſe the paſſing of an Act to this purpoſe?

The true reaſon is, becauſe they are wiſe enough to know, that a Law will certainly do it, as it hath done already, though they would perſwade others the contrary. And if it be doubted we have not Money enough in *England*. Beſides what I have ſaid in my former Treatiſe, as to the encreaſe of our Riches in general, I ſhall here give ſome further Reaſons of probability, which are the beſt that can be expected in this caſe, to prove that *we have now much more Money in* England *than we had twenty Years paſt*.

Notwithſtanding the ſeeming ſcarcity at preſent, if I ſhould look further back than twenty Years, the Argument would be ſtronger on my ſide, and the Proportion of the encreaſe of Money greater, and more Perſpicuous; but I ſhall confine my ſelf to that time which is within moſt Mens Memories.

1. We give generally now one third more Money with Apprentices than we did twenty Years paſt.

2. Notwithſtanding the decay and loſs of ſundry Trades and Manufactures, yet in the groſs we Ship off now one third part more of the Manufactures, as alſo Lead and Tin, than we did twenty Years paſt, which is a cauſe, as well as proof, of our Increaſe of Money.

If any doubt this, if they pleaſe to conſult Mr. *Dickins*, Surveyor of his Majeſties *Cuſtoms*, who is the beſt able I know living, and hath taken the moſt pains in theſe Calculations, he may be ſatisfactorily Reſolved.

3. Houſes new built in *London* yield twice the Rent they did before the Fire; and Houſes generally immediately before the Fire yielded about one fourth part more Rent than they did twenty Years paſt.

4. The ſpeedy and coſtly Buildings

of *London* is a Convincing (and to Strangers an Amazing) Argument of the plenty, and late encreaſe of Money in *England*.

5. We have now more than double the quantity of *Merchants* and *Shipping* we had twenty Years paſt.

6. The courſe of our Trade from the increaſe of our Money is ſtrangely altered within theſe twenty Years, moſt Payments from *Merchants* and *Shopkeepers* being now made with ready Money, whereas formerly the courſe of our general *Trade* run at three, ſix, nine, twelve and eighteen Months time.

But if this caſe be ſo clear, ſome may ask me, *How comes it to paſs that all ſorts of Men complain ſo much of the ſcarcity of* Money, *eſpecially in the Country?*

My Anſwers to this Query are, *viz.*

1. This proceeds from the Frailty and Corruption of Humane Nature, it being natural for Men to complain of the preſent, and commend the times paſt; ſo ſaid they of Old, *The former days were better than theſe*; and I can ſay in truth,

upon my own Memory, that Men did complain as much of the ſcarcity of Money ever ſince I knew the World as they do now; nay, the very ſame perſons that now complain of this, and commend that time.

2. And more particularly, *This Complaint proceeds from many mens finding themſelves uneaſie in the matters of their Religion*, it being natural for Men, when they are diſcontented at one thing, to complain of all, and principally to utter their Diſcontents and Complaints in thoſe things which are moſt popular. Thoſe that hate a Man for ſome one cauſe, will ſeldom allow of any thing that is good in him; and ſome that are angry with one perſon, or thing, will find fault with others that gave them no offence; like peeviſh Perſons that meeting diſcontent abroad, coming home, quarrel with their Wives, Children, Servants, *&c.*

3. And more eſpecially; this Complaint in the Country, proceeds from the late Practice of bringing up the

Tax-

Tax-Money in Wagons to *London*, which did doubtless cause a scarcity of Money in the Country.

4. And principally; *this seeming scarcity of Money proceeds from the Trade of Bankering*, which obstructs Circulation, aduanceth Usury, and renders it so easie, that most Men as soon as they can make up a Sum of 50 *l.* or a 100 *l.* send it into the *Gold-smith*; *Which doth and will occasion, while it lasts, that fatal pressing necessity for Money, so visible throughout the whole Kingdom, both to Prince and People.*

From what hath been last said, it appears the matter in *England* is prepared for the Abatement of Interest, which, as Sir *Henry Blunt* (an Honouracle Member of his Majesties Council of *Trade*) well said before the Lords at the debate, is the **Unum Magnum** towards the Prosperity of this Kingdom: It is a generative Good, and will bring many other good things with it.

I shall conclude with two or three Requests to the *Reader*.

1. That he would Read, and consider what he Reads, with an entire Love to his Country, and void of private Interests, and former ill-grounded impressions received into his Mind, to the Prejudice of this Principle.

2. That he would Read all (minding the Matter, not the Stile) before he make a Judgment.

3. That in all his Meditations upon these Principles, he would warily distinguish between the profit of the *Merchant* and the Gain of the *Kingdom*, which are so far from being always parrallels, that frequently they run counter one to the other, although most Men, by their Education and Business, having fixed their eye and aim wholly upon the former, do usually confound these two in their Thoughts and Discourses of *Trade*, or else mistake the former for the latter; from which false measures have proceeded many vulgar Errors in *Trade*, some whereof by reason of Mens frequent mistakings, as aforesaid, are become almost Proverbi-

al,

al, and often heard out of the Mouths, not only of the common People, but of Men that might know better, if they would duly consider the aforesaid distinction.

Some of the same common Proverbial Errors are, *viz.*

1. Vulgar Error; *We have too many* Merchants *already.*

2. *The Stock of* England *is too big for the Trade of* England.

3. *No Man should exercise two Callings.*

4. *Especially no* Shop-keeper *ought to be a* Merchant.

5. *Luxury and some Excess may be Profitable.*

6. *We have People enough, and more than we can employ.*

7. *To suffer Artificers to have as many Apprentices as they will, is to destroy Trade.*

8. *The admission of Strangers is to call in others to eat the Bread out of our own Mouths.*

9. *No Man ought to Live and Trade in a Corporation, that is not a Free man of the place.*

10. *Nor should any be Free-men, that are not the Sons of Free-men, or have served Seven Years Apprentiship.*

11. *It's better we Trade but for a hundred Pound at* 20 per cent, *profit, than for three hundred at* 10 per cent *profit, and so* pro rata.

12. *Our* Plantations *depopulate and consequently impoverish* England. With abundance more that might be named, but that many of them are occasionally hinted, and I hope them and others confuted in the following Discourse.

By what hath been said, and what follows, as well as by what most Men observe; *It is evident that this Kingdom is wonderfully fitted by the bounty of God Almighty for a great Progression in Wealth and Power:* And that the only means to arrive at both, or either of them, is to improve and advance Trade; and that the way to those Improvements is not hedged up with thorns, nor hidden from us in the dark, or intrigued with difficulties, but very natural and facile, if we would set about them

them, and begin the right way, casting off ſome of our old miſtaken Principles in Trade, which we inherit from our Anceſtors, who were Souldiers, Huntſ-men and Herdſ-men, and therefore neceſſarily unskilful in the Myſteries of, and Methods to improve Trade (though their natural parts were nothing inferior to ours) Trade being but a novel thing in *England*, comparatively to other parts of the World ; and in my opinion not yet advanced to the one fifth part of Improvement that this Land is capable of: and I think no true *Engliſh-man* will deny that the ſeaſon cries aloud to us, to be up and doing, before our Fields become un-occupied, and before the *Dutch* get too much the whip-hand of us, whom (in ſuch a caſe, were they freed from their *French* fears which they labour under at preſent) I fear we ſhould find as ſevere Task-Maſters, as ever the *Athenians* were to the leſſer Trading Cities of *Greece*.

Neither

Neither are the *Dutch* the only Neighbours we have at this time for Corrivals in Trade, but the *French King and King of* Sweden are now as active, circumſpect, induſtrious and Proſpective too in this Affair; and have, and are, ordering things as prudently for promoting thereof as the *Dutch* themſelves.

When I begun to Write this Treatiſe, I intended not to enlarge upon ſo many particulars, and the rather becauſe nothing can be ſaid for publick good, but will croſs the particular ends, as well as the opinions of many private Perſons, and ſtill the more is ſaid, the more are diſobliged; but my duty to my *Country* overcoming thoſe doubtful Conſiderations, I have adventured this ſecond time to expoſe my Conceptions to publick Cenſure, with this Confidence, that after theſe Principles have ſuffered the accuſtomary Perſecution of Tongues and Pens, naturally and conſtantly accompanying all new Propoſals for a while, they will at

length,

length, the most, if not all of them, or something very like them, come to be generally received and honoured with the publick Sanction, by being passed into Laws (gradually, not at once) concerning the time whereof I am not careful, but for my Country's sake, *I could wish it might be shortned.*

THE
CONTENTS.

First, A *Discourse concerning Trade*, &c.

Chap.

A

A

DISCOURSE

Concerning

Trade, &c.

THE Prodigious increase of the *Netherlands* in their Domestick and Foreign Trade, Riches, and multitude of Shipping, is the envy of the present, and may be the wonder of all future Generations: And yet the means whereby they have thus advanced themselves, are sufficiently obvious, and in a great measure imitable by most other Nations; but more easily by us of this Kingdom of *England*; which I shall endeavour to demonstrate in the following Discourse.

Some of the said means by which they have advanced their Trade, and thereby improved their Estates, are the following.

First, They have in their greatest *Councils of State and War*, Trading Merchants, that have lived abroad in most parts of the

World; who have not only the Theoretical Knowledge, but the Practical Experience of Trade, by whom Laws and Orders are contrived, and Peaces with foreign Princes projected, to the great Advantage of their Trade.

Secondly, Their Law of *Gavel-kind*, whereby all their Children possess an equal share of their Fathers Estates after their decease, and so are not left to wrestle with the world in their Youth, with inconsiderable assistance of Fortune, as most of our youngest Sons of Gentlemen in *England* are, who are bound Apprentices to Merchants.

Thirdly, Their exact making of all their Native Commodities, and packing of their *Herrings*, *Cod-fish*, and all other Commodities, which they send abroad in great quantities; the consequence whereof is, That the repute of their said Commodities abroad continues always good, and the Buyers will accept of them by the Marks, without opening; whereas the Fish which our *English* make in *New-found-Land* and *New-England*, and *Herrings* at *Yarmouth*, often prove false and deceitfully made; and our *Pilchards* from the *West Country* false packed, seldom containing the quantity for which the Hogsheads are marked, in which they are packed.

And in *England* the attempts which our

Fore-

Fore-fathers made for regulating of Manufactures, when left to the execution of ſome particular Perſon, in a ſhort time reſolved bnt into a Tax upon the Commodity, without reſpect to the goodneſs thereof; as moſt notoriouſly appears in the buſineſs of the AULNAGE, which doubtleſs our Predeceſſors intended for a ſcrutiny into the goodneſs of the Commodity; and to that purpoſe a Seal was invented, as a ſignal that the Commodity was made according to the Statutes; which *Seals*, it is ſaid, may now be bought by Thouſands, and put upon what the buyers pleaſe.

Fourthly, Their giving great incouragement and immunities to the Inventors of New Manufactures, and the Diſcoverers of any New Myſteries in Trade, and to thoſe that ſhall bring the Commoditis of other Nations firſt in uſe and practice amongſt them; for which the Author never goes without his due Reward allowed him at the Publick Charge.

Fifthly, Their Contriving and Building of great Ships to Sail with ſmall Charge, not above one third of what we are at, for Ships of the ſame Burthen in *England*; and compelling their ſaid Ships (being of ſmall Force) to Sail always in Fleets, to which in all times of Danger they allow *Convoy*.

Sixthly, Their parcimonious and thrifty living, which is so extraordinary that a Merchant of one hundred thousand pound Estate with them, will scarce spend so much *per Annum*, as one of Fifteen Hundred Pounds Estate in *London*.

Seventhly, The Education of their Children, as well Daughters as Sons; all which, be they of never so great Quality or *Estate*, they always take care to bring up to write perfect good Hands, and to have the full knowledge and use of *Arithmetick* and *Merchants Accounts*; the well understanding and practice whereof, doth strangly infuse into most that are the owners of that Quality, of either Sex, not only an Ability for Commerce of all kinds, but a strong aptitude, love and delight in it; and in regard the Women are as knowing therein as the Men, it doth incourage their Husbands to hold on in their Trades to their dying days, knowing the capacity of their Wives to get in their Estates, and carry on their Trades after their Death: Whereas if a Merchant in *England* arrive at any considerable Estate, he commonly with-draws his Estate from Trade, before he comes near the confines of old Age; reckoning that if God should call him out of the World, while the main of his Estate is engaged abroad in Trade, he must

lose

lose one third of it, through the unexperience and unaptness of his Wife to such Affairs; and so it usually falls out.

Besides, it hath been observed in the nature of *Arithmetick*, that, like other parts of the *Mathematicks*, it doth not only improve the *Rational Faculties*, but inclines those that are expert in it to Thriftiness and good Husbandry, and prevents both Husbands and Wives in some measure from running out of their Estates, when they have it always ready in their Heads what their expences do amount to, and how soon by that course their ruin must overtake them.

Eighthly, The lowness of their *Customs*, and the height of their *Excise*, which is certainly the most equal and indifferent *Tax* in the World, and least prejudicial to any People, as might be made appear, were it the subject of this Discourse.

Ninthly, The careful providing for and employing their Poor, which, it is easie to demonstrate, can never be done in *England* comparatively to what it is with them, while it's left to the care of every Parish to look after their own only.

Tenthly, Their use of BANKS, which are of so immense advantage to them, that some not without good grounds have estimated the Profit of them to the Publick, to amount to at least one Million of Pounds *Sterling per Annum.*

Eleventhly, Their *Tolleration of different Opinions in matters of Religion*; by reason whereof many *Industrious People* of other Countries, *that dissent from the Established Government of their own Churches, resort to them with their Families and Estates, and after a few Years Co-habitation with them, become of the same common Interest.*

Twelfthly, Their *Law-Merchants,* by which all Controversies between *Merchant* and *Tradesmen* are decided in three or four days time, and that not at the fourtieth part (*I might say in many cases not the hundreth part*) of the Charge they are with us.

Thirteenthly, The Law that is in use among them for *Transferrence of Bills for Debt* from one Man to another: This is of extraordinary advantage to them in their Commerce; by means whereof, they can turn their Stocks twice or thrice in Trade, for once that we can in *England*; for that having sold our Foreign Goods here, we cannot buy again to advantage, till we are possest of our Money; which it may be we shall be six, nine, or twelve Months in recovering; and if what we sell be considerable, it is a good Man's work all the Year to be following Vintners and Shop-keepers for Money.

Money. Whereas, were the Law for transferring Bills in practice with us, we could presently after Sale of our Goods, dispose of our Bills, and close up our Accounts. To do which, the Advantage, Ease, and Accommodations it would be to Trade, is so great that none but *Merchants* that have lived where that custom is in use, can value to its due proportion.

Fourteenthly, Their keeping up PUBLICK REGISTERS of all Lands and Houses, Sold or Mortgaged, whereby many chargeable *Law-Suits* are prevented, and the Securities of Lands and Houses rendred indeed, such as we commonly call them, REAL SECURITY.

Lastly, The *lowness of Interest of Money with them*, which in Peaceable Times exceeds not 3 *per cent per annum*; and is now during this War with *England* not above 4 *per cent* at most.

Some more Particulars might be added, and those aforesaid further improved, were it my Purpose to Discourse at large of Trade. But seeing most of the former Particulars are observed and granted by all Men that make it any part of their Business to inspect the true *Natures* and *Principles of Trade*; but the last is not so much as taken notice of by the most Ingenious, to be any

Cause of the great encreafe of the Riches and Commerce of that People.

I shall therefore in this Paper confine my self to write Principally my Observations touching that, *viz.*

The Profit *That People* have received, and any other may receive, by reducing the Interest of Money to a very low rate.

This, in my poor opinion, is the **Causa Causans** of all the other Causes of the Riches of that People; and that if Interest of Money were with us reduced to the same Rate it is with them, it would in a short time render us as Rich and Considerable in Trade as they now are; and consequently be of greater Damage to them, and Advantage to us, than can happen by the Issue of this present War, though the success of it should be as good as we can wish, except it end in their total Ruine and Extirpation.

To illustrate this, let us Impartially search our Books, and enquire what the state and condition of this Kingdom was, as to Trade and Riches, before any Law concerning Interest of money was made: The first whereof, that I can find, was *Anno* 1545. and we shall be informed that the Trade of *England* then was inconsiderable, and the Merchants very mean and few: And that afterwards, *viz. Anno* 1635. within Ten Years after

after Intereſt was brought down to Eight *per cent*, there was more Merchants to be found upon the *Exchange* worth each one thouſand Pounds and upwards, than were in the former Days, *viz*. before the Year 1600. to be found worth one hundred Pounds each.

And now ſince Intereſt hath been for about twenty Years at ſix *per cent*, notwithſtanding our long civil Wars, and the great Complaints of the deadneſs of Trade, there are more Men to be found upon the *Exchange* now worth Ten Thouſand Pounds Eſtates, than were then of One Thouſand Pounds.

And if this be doubted, let us ask the Aged, whether Five Hundred Pounds Portion with a Daughter Sixty Years ago, were not eſteemed a lager Portion than Two Thouſand Pounds is now: And whether Gentlewomen in thoſe days would not eſteem themſelves well Cloathed in a Searge Gown, which a Chamber-Maid now will be aſham'd to be ſeen in: Whether our Citizens and middle ſort of Gentry now are not more Rich in Cloaths, Plate, Jewels, and Houſhold-Goods, *&c.* than the beſt ſort of Knights and Gentry were in thoſe days; and whether our beſt ſorts of Knights and Gentry now do not exceed by much in thoſe things the

the Nobility of *England* Sixty Years past: Many of whom then would not go to the Price of a whole Sattin-Doublet: The *Embroiderer* being yet living, who hath assured me he hath made many Hundreds of them for the Nobility with Canvas Backs.

Which way ever we take our measures, to me it seems evident, that since our first abatement of Interest, the Riches and Splendor of this Kindom is increased to above Four (I may say, above Six) times so much as it was.

We have now almost One Hundred Coaches for one we had formerly, We with ease can pay a greater *Tax* now in One Year, than our Fore-fathers could in Twenty.

Our *Customs* are very much improved, I Believe above the Proportion aforesaid, of Six to One, which is not so much in advance of the Rates of Goods, as by encrease of the Bulk of Trade; for though some Foreign Commodities are advanced, others of our Native Commodities and Manufactures are considerably abated, by the last Book of Rates.

I can my self remember since there were not at *London* used so many Wharfs or Keys for the Landing of Merchants Goods, by at least one third part, as now there are; and those that were then could scarce have Im-

ployment

ployment for half what they could do; and now notwithstanding one third more used to the same purpose, they are all too little in a time of Peace, to Land the Goods at, that come to *London*.

If we look into the Country, we shall find *Lands* as much Improved since the abatement of Interest, as Trade, *&c.* in Cities; that now yielding Twenty Years Purchase, which then would not have Sold for above Eight or Ten at most.

Besides, the Rent of Farms have been for these last 30 Years much advanced; and although they have for these three or four last Years fallen, that hath no respect at all to the lowness of Interest at present, nor to the other mistaken Reasons which are commonly assigned for it.

But Principally to the vast Improvement of *Ireland*, since a great part of it was lately Possessed by the Industrous *English*, who were Soldiers in the late *Army*; and the late great Land-Taxes.

More might be said; but the Premises being considered, I Judge, will sufficiently demonstrate how greatly this Kingdom of *England* hath been advanced in all respects for these last Fifty Years: And that the Abatement of Interest hath been the cause thereof, to me seems most probable; because as

it

it appears it hath been in *England*, ſo I find it is at this day in all *Europe*, and other parts of the World: Inſomuch that to know whether any Country be Rich or Poor, or in what Proportion it is ſo, no other Queſtion needs be Reſolved, but this, *viz. What Intereſt do they pay for Money?* Near home we ſee it evidently, in *Scotland* and *Ireland*, where Ten and Twelve *per cent* is paid for Intereſt, the People are Poor and Deſpicable, their Perſons ill Cloathed, their Houſes worſe Provided, and Money intollerably Scarce, notwithſtanding they have great plenty of all Proviſions; nor will their Land yield above 8 or 10 Years Purchaſe at moſt.

In *France*, where Money is at Seven *per cent*; their Lands will yield about Eighteen Years Purchaſe; and the Gentry who may Poſſeſs Lands, live in good Condition, though the *Peaſants* are little better than Slaves, becauſe they can Poſſeſs nothing but at the will of others.

In *Italy* Money will not yield above three *per cent*, to be left out upon real Security; there the People are Rich, full of Trade, well Attired, and their Lands will Sell at 35 to 40 Years Purchaſe; and that it is ſo or better with them in *Holland*, is too manifeſt.

In *Spain* the uſual Intereſt is Ten and Twelve *per cent*, and there, notwithſtanding

ing they have the only Trade in the World for Gold and Silver, Money is no where more ſcarce; the People Poor, Deſpicable, and void of Commerce, other than ſuch as *Engliſh*, *Dutch*, *Italians*, *Jews*, and other Foreigners bring to them; who are to them in effect, but as Leeches, who ſuck their Blood and Vital Spirits from them.

I might urge many other Inſtances of this Nature, not only out of *Chriſtendom*, but from under the *Turks* Dominions, *East-India* and *America*: But every Man by his Experience in Foreign Countries, may eaſily inform himſelf, whether this Rule do univerſally hold True or not: For my own part, to ſatisfie my own Curioſity, I have for ſome Years, as occaſion offered, diligently enquired of all my Acquaintance that had knowledge of Foreign Countries, and I can truly ſay, that I never found it to fail in any particular Inſtance.

Now if upon what hath been ſaid, it be granted that, *De facto*, this Kingdom be Richer at leaſt Four-fold (I might ſay, Eight-fold) than it was before any Law for Intereſt was made, and that *all Countries are at this day Richer or Poorer in an exact Proportion to what they pay, and have uſually paid for the Intereſt of Money*; It remains that we enquire carefully, whether the Abatement of Intereſt be

in

in Truth the Cause of the Riches of any Country, or only the Concomitant or Effect of the Riches of a Country; in which seems to lie the Intricacy of this Question.

To satisfie my self herein, I have taken all Opportunities to Discourse this Point, with the most Ingenious Men I had the Honour to be known to, and have search'd for, and Read all the Books that I could ever hear were Printed against the Abatement of Interest, and seriously considered all the Arguments and Objections used by them against it: All which have tended to confirm me in this Opinion, which I humbly offer to the Consideration of wiser Heads, *viz.* **That the Abatement of Interest is the Cause of the Prosperity and Riches of any Nation,** *and that the bringing down of Interest in this Kingdom from Six to Four or Three* per cent, *will necessarily, in less than Twenty Years time, double the Capital Stock of the Nation.*

The most material Objections I have met with against it, are as follows:

Object. 1. *To abate Interest, will cause the* Dutch, *and other People that have Money put out at Interest in* England, *by their Friends and Factors, to call home their Estates, and consequently will occasion a great scarcity and want of Money amongst us.*

To

To this I anſwer, That if Intereſt be brought but to Four *per cent*, no *Dutch-man* will call in his Money that is out upon good Security in *England*, becauſe he cannot make above three *per cent* of it upon Intereſt at home. But if they ſhould call home all the Money they have with us at Intereſt, it would be better for us than if they did it not; for *the Borrower is always a Slave to the Lender*, and ſhall be ſure to be always kept Poor, while the other is Fat and Full: HE THAT USETH A STOCK THAT IS NONE OF HIS OWN, BEING FORCED FOR THE UPHOLDING HIS REPUTATION TO LIVE TO THE FULL, IF NOT ABOVE THE PROPORTION OF WHAT HE DOTH SO USE, WHILE THE LENDER POSSESSING MUCH, AND USING LITTLE OR NONE, LIVES ONLY AT THE CHARGE OF WHAT HE USETH, AND NOT OF WHAT HE HATH.

Beſides, if with this Law for Abatement of Intereſt, a Law for *Transferring Bills of Debt* ſhould paſs, we ſhould not miſs the *Dutch* Money, were it ten times as much as it is amongſt us; for that ſuch a Law will certainly ſupply the defect of at leaſt one half of all the ready Money we have in uſe in the Nation.

Object.

Object. 2. *If Interest be Abated, Land must rise in Purchase, and consequently Rents, then the Fruits of the Land; and so all things will be Dear, and how shall the Poor Live?* &c.

Answ. To this I say, If it follow that the Fruits of our Land, in consequence of such a Law for Abatement of Interest, grow generally Dear, it is an evident demonstration that our People grow Richer; for generally, *Where-ever Provisions are for continuance of years dear in any Country, the People are Rich; and where they are most cheap throughout the World, for the most part the People are very Poor.*

And for our own Poor in *England*, it is observed, *That they live better in the Dearest Countries for Provisions than in the Cheapest, and better in a Dear Year than in a Cheap,* (especially in relation to the Publick Good) for that in a Cheap Year they will not work above two Days in a Week; their Humour being such, that they will not provide for a hard Time, but just work so much and no more, as may maintain them in that mean Condition to which they have been Accustomed.

Object. 3. *If Interest be Abated, Usurers will call in their Money; so what shall Gentlemen do whose Estates are Mortgaged?* &c.

Answ. I answer, That when they know they can make no more of their Money by taking

taking out of one, and putting it in another hand, they will not be so foreward as they threaten, to alter that security they know is good, for another that may be bad: Or if they should do it, our Laws are not so severe but that Gentlemen may take time to dispose of part of their Land, which immediatly after such a Law will yield them thirty years purchase at least, and much better it is for them so to do, than to abide longer under that consuming Plague of Usury, which hath insensibly destroyed very many of the best Families in *England*, as well of our Nobility as Gentry.

Object. 4. *As Interest is now at six* per cent, *the Kings Majesty upon any emergency can hardly be supplyed; and if it should be reduced to four* per cent, *how shall the King find a considerable sum of Money to be lent him by his People.*

Answ. I answer, The abatement of Interest to the People, is the abatement of interest to the King, when he hath occasion to take up Money: For what is borrowed of the *City of London*, or other *Bodies Politick*, nothing can be demanded but the legal Interest; and if the King have occasion to take up Money of private Persons, being his Maesty, according to good right, is above the common course of Law, the King must, and always hath given more than the legal Rate,

As for Instance, The legal Rate is now six *per cent*, but his Majesty, or such as have disposed of his Majesties *Exchequer Tallies*, have been said to give ten and twelve in some cases; and if the legal Rate were ten, his Majesty might probably give thirteen or fourteen: So if Interest be brought to four *per cent*, his Majesty in such cases as he now gives ten must give six or seven; by which his Majesty would have a clear advantage.

Object. 5. *If Interest be abated, it will be a great prejudice to Widows and Orphans, who have not Knowledge and Abilities to improve their Estates otherwise.*

Answ. I answer, that by our Law now, *Heirs* and *Orphans* can recover no Interest from their Parents *Executors*, except it be left fully and absolutely to the Executors to dispose and put out Money at the discretion of the *Executors*, for the profit and loss of the *Heirs* and *Orphans*: And if it be so left to the *Executors* discretion, they may improve the Monies left them in Trade, or purchase of Lands and Leases, as well as by Interest: Or when not, the damage such *Heirs* and *Orphans* will sustain in their minority (being but two *per cent*) is inconsiderable, in respect of the great advantage will accrew to the Nation in general, by such abatement of Interest.

Besides,

Besides, when such a Law is made & in use, all Men will so take care in their Life to provide for, and educate their *Children*, and instruct their *Wives*, as that no prejudice can happen thereby; as we see there doth not in *Holland* and *Italy*, and other places where Interest is so low.

Having now offered my thoughts in answer to the aforesaid Objections; it will not be amiss that we inquire who will be advantaged, and who will receive prejudice, in case such a Law be made.

First, His Majesty, as hath been said in answer to that Objection, will, when he hath occasion, take up Money on better terms: Besides which, He will receive a great Augmentation to his Revenue thereby, all his *Lands* being immediately worth, after the making such a Law, double to what they were before; his *Customs* will be much increased by the increase of Trade, which must necessarily insue upon the making such a Law.

The *Nobility* and *Gentry*, whose Estates lie mostly in Land, may presently upon all they have, *instead of Fifty, write one Hundred.*

The *Merchants* and *Tradesmen, who bear the Heat and Burden of the Day* (most of our Trade being carried on by young Men that take up Money at Interest) will find their

Youk ſit lighter upon their *Shoulders*, and be incouraged to go on with greater alacrity in their Buſineſs.

Our *Mariners*, *Shipwrights*, *Porters*, *Cloathiers*, *Packers*, and all ſorts of *Labouring People* that depend on Trade, will be more conſtantly and fully employed.

Our *Farmers* ſell the Product of their Lands at better Rates. And whereas our Neighbours in the *Netherlands* (whom in regard of the largeneſs of their Stocks, and Experiences, the Sons continually ſucceeding the Fathers in Trade to many Generations, we may not unfitly in this caſe term *Sons of Anack, and Men of renown*) againſt whom we fight, *Dwarfs* and *Pigmies* in *Stocks and experience*, being *younger Brothers of Gentlemen* that ſeldom have above one thouſand Pounds, ſometimes not two Hundred, to begin the World with: Inſtead I ſay of ſuch young Men and ſmall Stocks (if this Law paſs) we ſhall bring forth our *Sampſons* and *Goliahs* in Stocks, ſubtilty, and experience in Trade to coap with our potent Adverſaries on the other ſide; there being to every Mans knowledge that underſtands the *Exchange of London*, divers *Engliſh Merchants* of large Eſtates, which have not much paſt their middle-Age, and yet have wholly left off their Trades, having found the ſweetneſs vhich if that should abate, must *hands to the Plough*, (which they hold and govern now as ever) engage them to train up their me way, because it will not be ake them *Country Gentlemen* as ıen Lands sell at thirty or four-:hase.

fferers by such a Law, I know e Persons that live at as little abour, *Neither scattering by their the Poor may Glean any thing af- Working with their hands or heads r Wax or Hony to the common Kingdom; but swelling their own sweat of other Mens Brows and es of other Mens Brains: And how is for a Nation, to suffer* **Idle- s the Breasts of Industry;** nonstration. And if it be gran- these will be the effects of an f Interest, then I think it is , *that the abatement of Interest e enriching of a Nation; and con- been one great cause of the Riches and* Italians, *and the encrease of ir own Kingdom in these last fifty*

rgument to prove which, we m the nature of *Interest* it self, which is of ſo prodigious a Multiplying nature, that it muſt of neceſſity make the Lenders monſtruous rich (if they live at any moderate expence) and the Borrowers extream Poor: A memorable inſtance whereof, we have in *Old Audly* deceaſed, who did wiſely obſerve, *That one Hundred Pounds only, put out at Intereſt at ten* per cent, *doth in ſeventy years (which is but the Age of a Man) increaſe to above one hundred thouſand Pounds:* And if the Advantage be ſo great to the Lender, the loſs muſt be greater to the Borrower, who (as hath been ſaid) lives at a much larger Expence. And as it is between private Perſons, ſo between Nation and Nation, that have Communication one with another. For whether the Subjects of one Nation lend Money to the Subjects of another, or Trade with them for Goods, the effect is the ſame. As for example, a *Dutch Merchant* that hath but four or five Thouſand Pounds clear Stock of his own, can eaſily borrow and have credit for fifteen Thouſand Pounds more at 3 *per cent* at Home; with which, whether he Trade or put it to uſe in *England*, or any Country where Intereſt of Money is high, he muſt neceſſarily (without very evil Accidents attend him) in a very few years, treble his own Capital.

This diſcovers the true cauſe, why the

Sugar-

Sugar-Bakers of *Holland* can afford to give a greater price for *Barbadoes Sugars* in *London*, besides the second Freight and Charges upon them between *England* and *Holland*, and yet grow exceeding Rich upon their Trade: Whereas our *Sugar-Bakers* in *London*, that buy Sugars here at their own Doors, before such additional Freight and Charges come upon them, can scarce live upon their Callings, ours here paying for a good share of their Stocks six *per cent*, and few of them employ in their Sugar-works above six to ten Thousand Pounds at most: Whereas in *Holland* they employ twenty, thirty, to fourty thousand Pounds Stock in a *Sugar-House*, paying but three *per cent* at most for what they take up at Interest, to fill up their said Stocks; which is sometimes half, sometimes three quarters of their whole Stocks. And as it is with this Trade, the same Rules hold throughout all other Trades whatsoever. And for us to say, if the *Dutch* put their Money to Interest among us, we shall have the advantage by being full and flush of Coin at Home; it is a mear *Chymera*, and so far from an Advantage, that is is an extream Loss, rendring us only in the condition of a young Gallant, that hath newly Mortgaged his Land, and with the Money thereby raised, stuffs his

Pockets and looks big for a time, not considering that the draught of Cordial he hath received, though it be at-present grateful to his Palat, doth indeed prey upon his vital Spirits; and will in a short time render the whole body of his Estate in a deep Consumption, if not wholly consumed: Besides, whatever Money the *Dutch* lend us, they always keep one end of the Chain at home in their own Hands; by which they can pull back when they please their *Lean Kine* which they send here to be fatted.

This makes me conclude that *Moses* (that wise Legislator) in his forbidding the *Jews* to lend Money at use one to another, and permitting them to lend their Money to *Strangers*, ordained that Law as much to a *Political* as a *Religious intent*; knowing that by the latter they should Enrich their own Nation, and by the former no publick Good could insue; the consequence being only to impoverish one *Jew* to make another Rich.

This likewise takes off the wonder how the People of *Israel*, out of so small a Territory as they possessed, could upon all occasions set forth such vast and numerous Armies (almost incredible) as all Histories, Sacred and Prophane, report they did; which is neither impossible nor strange to any that have well considered the effects of their

their Laws concerning *Usury*, which were sufficient *to make any barren Land fruitful, and a fruitful Land an entire Garden*, which by consequence would maintain ten times the number of Inhabitants that the same Tract of Land would do where no such Laws were.

To conclude, it is (I think) agreed on by all, That *Merchants*, *Artificers*, *Farmers of Land*, and such as depend on them (which for brevity-sake we may here include under one of these General terms, *viz. Sea-men, Fisher-men, Breeders of Cattle, Gardners*, &c.) are the three sorts of People which by their Study and Labour do principally, if not only, bring in Wealth to a Nation from abroad; other kinds of People, *viz. Nobility, Gentry, Lawyers, Physicians, Scholars* of all sorts, and *Shop-keepers*, do only hand it from one to another at home. And if abatement of Interest (besides the general benefit it brings to all, except the *Griping Dronish Usurer*) will add new Life and Motion to those most profitable Engines of the Kingdom, as (I humbly suppose) will be manifest upon serious consideration of what hath been said; then I think it will be out of doubt, that abatement of Interest is the Cause of increase of the Trade and Riches of any Kingdom.

Suppli-

Suppliment.

THE fore-going Discourse I Wrote in the Sickness-Summer, at my Country-Habitation, not then intending to publish it, but only to communicate it to some Honourable and Ingenious Friends of the present *Parliament*, who were pleased to take Copies of it, for their own deliberate Consideration and digestion of the principles therein asserted; which at first were strange to them, as I expect they will be to most others, till they have spent some time in thinking on them; after which I doubt not but all Men will be convinced of the *Truth* of them, that have not some private Interest of their own against them, *external to the general Good of the Kingdom*. For sure I am they have a *Foundation in Nature*, and that according to the excellent Sir *William Petty*'s Observation in his late Discourse concerning Taxes, *Res nolunt male Admiministrari:* Nature must and will have its course, the matter in *England* is pre-

pared

pared for an Abatement of Intereſt, and it cannot long be obſtructed; and, after the next abatement, who ever lives fourty years longer ſhall ſee a ſecond Abatement; for we ſhall never ſtand on even ground in Trade with the *Dutch*, till Intereſt be the ſame with us, as it is with them.

His Majeſty was graciouſly pleaſed at the opening of the laſt Seſſion of this *Parliament*, to propoſe to the Conſideration of both Houſes, the Ballancing of the Trade of the Nation: to effect which, in my opinion, the Abatement of Intereſt is the firſt and Principal *Engine* which ought to be ſet on work; which notwithſtanding, I ſhould not have preſumed to expoſe it to publick cenſure on my own ſingle opinion, if I had not had the concurrence of much better Judgements than my own; having never ſeen any thing in Print for it (though much againſt it) until the latter end of *January* laſt; at which time, a Friend whom I had often diſcourſed with upon this Subject, met with, by accident, a ſmall Tract to the ſame purpoſe, wrote near fifty years ago, which he gave me, and I have for publick Good thought fit to annex it hereunto, *verbatim.*

The *Author* of the ſaid Tract, by the ſtile thereof, ſeems to have been a *Country-Gentleman*

tleman, and my Education hath moſtly been that of a *Merchant*, ſo I hope that, going together, they may, in ſome meaſure ſupply the defects of each other.

Another reaſon that induced me to the Printing of them together, is, becauſe what he Wrote then, would be the conſequences of the Abatement of Intereſt from ten to ſix *per cent*, I have I think fully proved to the conviction of all Men not wilfully blind, have been the real effects thereof, and that to a greater proportion than he did premiſe; every Paragraph whereof was writ by me, and Copies thereof delivered to ſeveral worthy Members of this *Parliament*, many Months before ever I ſaw or heard of this, or any thing elſe Writ or Printed to the like purpoſe.

What I have aimed at in the whole, is the good of my Native Country, otherwiſe I had not buſied my ſelf about it, for I want not employment ſufficient of my own, nor have reaſon to be out of love with that I have.

The ſeveral Particulars in the beginning of this Treatiſe, relating to Trade, I have only hinted in general terms; hoping that ſome abler Pen, will hereafter be incited for the ſervice of his *King* and *Country*, to enlarge more particularly upon them.

Before

Before I conclude, though I have studied brevity in the whole, I cannot omit the inserting of one *Objection* more, which I have lately met with, to the main design of this Treatise, *viz*,

Object. It is said that the lowness of Interest of Money in *Holland*, is not the EFFECT OF LAWS, but proceeds only FROM THEIR ABUNDANCE THEREOF, for that in *Holland* there is no Law limiting the rate of Usury.

Answ. I answer, that it may be true, that in *Holland* there hath not lately been any Law, to limit Usury to the present rate it is now at, *i. e.* three or four *per cent*; although most certain it is, that many years since, there was a Law that did limit it to five or six at most: And by consequence, there would be a renewing of that Law to a lesser rate, were it necessary at this time; *It having always been the Policy of that People to keep down the Interest of their Money, three or four* per cent, *under the rate of what is usually paid in their Neighbouring Countries*, which (being now naturally done) it is needless to use the *Artificial Stratagem of a Law to establish*.

Answ. 2. Although they have no Law expresly, limiting Interest at present, yet they have other Laws which we cannot yet arrive

to,

to, which do effect the same thing among them, and would do the like among us, if we could have them: One whereof is, their ascertaining REAL SECURITIES by their PUBLICK REGISTERS: For we see evidently, Money is not so much wanting in *England* as Securities, which Men account infallible; a remarkable Instance whereof is, the *East-India Company*, who can and do take up what Money they please for four *per cent* at any time.

Another Law is, Their constitution of BANKS and LUMBARDS, whereby private Persons that have but tollerable credit may be supplyed at easie Rates from the State.

A third, and very considerable one, is Their *Law for Transferring Bills of Debt*, mentioned in the beginning of this Discourse.

A fourth, which is a Custom, and in effect may be here to our purpose accounted as a Law, is the extraordinary Frugality used in all their *Publick Affairs*, which in their greatest Extremities have been such, as not to compel them to give above four *per cent* for the loan of Money. Whereas it is said, *His Majesty in some Cases of exigency, where the National Supplies have not come in to answer the present Emergencies of Affairs, hath been inforced to give above the usual Rates to*

Gold-

Gold-Smiths; and that encouraged them to take up great Sums from private Perſons at the full rate of ſix *per cent*, whereas formerly they uſually gave but four *per cent* otherwiſe, in humane probability, Money would have fallen of it ſelf to four *per cent*.

But again to conclude, *Every Nation does proceed according to peculiar methods of their own in the Tranſactions of their publick Affairs and Law-making:* And in this Kingdom it hath always been the Cuſtom *to Reduce the rate of Intereſt by a Law, when Nature had prepared the matter fit for ſuch an alteration, as now I ſay it hath.* By a Law it was reduced from an unlimited rate, to ten; and afterwards from ten to eight; after that from eight to ſix. And through the Bleſſing of Almighty God, this Kingdom hath found, as I think I have fully proved, and every Mans Experience will witneſs, prodigious ſucceſs and advantage thereby. And I doubt not, through the like Bleſſing of God Almighty, but this Generation will find the like great and good effects, by the reduction of it from ſix to four, which is now at the Birth. And that the next Generation will yet ſee far greater Advantage by bringing it from four to three *per cent*.

[illegible]

A

TRADE AND Intereſt of Money CONSIDERED, &c.

CHAP. I.

A ſhort Reply to a Treatiſe, Entituled, *Intereſt of Money Miſtaken*.

THERE was never any thing Propounded for Publick Good, that did not meet with Oppoſition ariſing ſometimes from the different Apprehenſions of Men, in regard of the way, who yet have the ſame deſign as to the end; ſometimes from a diſlike of the Perſon Propounding, or the Humour of ſuch as would have nothing brought into the World but by

 their

their own Midwifery; and are therefore only displeased with a thing, because they were not the first Proposers of it themselves; sometimes from a more inveterate and corrupt Principle of wishing things worse, because they are not well, hating that any thing should be reformed, because they cannot bring all things to the Figure of their own Fancies; and sometimes from other bye Respects and private Interests.

Whether any, or which of these hath moved my *Opposer*, I will not here determine, because I know him not, but leaving that to the Judgment of the Impartial Reader, if the Gentleman's love to his Country be such as he Professeth, and equal with mine, I shall not doubt but after a more serious Examination of the Matter, he will agree with me in the very thing desired.

In the beginning of his Treatise he recites nineteen *Observations* of mine, as means whereby the *Dutch* have encreased their Trade and Riches; And Page 9. seems to approve of them all, saying as I told him as also he doth, Page 22. *That more might be added*; but is not so kind to his Country to let us know what they are; which if he had done, would have been more agreeable to his pretended Candor, and as well of use to his Country, as an evidence of his

ow-

own Sufficiency; it being a much easier thing to cavil at what other Men have done, than to present the World with any thing new and material of our own.

Page 10. (passing over many others) he Quarrels at that Facetious Instance of *Noble-Men's wearing in former times Sattin Doublets with Canvas Backs*, which is the most inconsiderable instance of many; yet, upon the whole he concludes with me, *That we are much Richer now than we were before any Law for Interest was made, and that we have grown Richer since the Abatement of Interest from* 10 *to* 8 per cent; *and yet more Rich since it was Abated from* 8 *to* 6 per cent; which Page 10. he Confesseth, and Page 11. he Implicitely Confesseth, and Page 14. Expresly, *That according to the more or less Interest any Country pays for Money, the Richer or Poorer it is.* I am glad we are thus far agreed, and that my Opposer is so well Instructed, hoping I shall with the less difficulty perswade him to a perfect Understanding of the Principle in Controversie, wherein as yet I think it will appear he is no great Master.

But before I enter into the Matter, I must tell the Gentleman, he hath no cause to boast as to that particular Instance concerning Noble Men's former meaner Cloathing; for what I thence Inferred was certainly true, as to the time I ſpoke of, which was of a time within the memory of a Man then living, ſince Trade was Introduced into this Kingdom; which he endeavours to overthrow by an Inſtance out of thoſe times, when Noble-men kept Multitudes of Retainers about 200 Years paſt, *viz.* Before *Henry* the 7th's time, and before Trade was underſtood in *England*, which I think is nothing to this purpoſe. Page 11. The Gentleman reciting my Anſwer to that Objection, *That if Intereſt be Abated, the* Dutch *will call home their Money*; To which I replied, That if they ſhould, it would be better for us, *The Borrower being always a Slave to the Lender*; which, he ſaith, *Is no more in the caſe of* Engliſh *and* Dutch, *than in that of* Engliſh *and* Engliſh. And Page 12. at the beginning, he ſaith, *That I have diſcovered my deſign of Engroſſing all Trade into the Hands of a few Rich Merchants, who have Money enough of their own to Trade with, to the excluding all Young Men that want it.*

In which two Aſſertions I appeal to all Rational Men, whether the Gentleman be not in a very great Error, as to the very Nature of the Principle he Diſcourſeth? For if one *Engliſh-man* lend to another, be the Intereſt high or low, between them two nothing is got or loſt to the Nation; whereas if a *Dutch* Man lend Money to an *English* Man, he at length carries home both Principal and Intereſt; which Intereſt, be it more or leſs, is a clear loſs to the Nation; which is ſo evident, that I hope my Oppoſer, when he hath thought upon it again, will not upbraid me for begging the Queſtion, becauſe I trouble not the Reader with the particular Proof of theſe things which I hear no Man deny, and therefore conclude, every Man will grant: For whether Snow be white is not to be disputed.

In his Second Aſſertion likewiſe, That the Abatement of Intereſt tends to the engroſſing of Trade into a few Rich Men's hands, to the excluding of Young Men, I appeal to the Judgment of all Underſtanding Merchants and Rational Men, whether the Gentleman be not miſerably miſtaken? And whether the never-failing Effects of a high Intereſt, all the World over, be not to Enrich a few greatly, and Impoveriſh the generality of Traders? So it is in *Turkey*, where Intereſt is at 20 *per cent*, and upwards, if we may believe thoſe honeſt and worthy *Turkey* Merchants, who are now upon the *Exchange*, and have lived long in that Country; and ſo it was with us here, when Intereſt was at 10 *per cent*, and upwards, as I have already demonſtrated by the inſtances of *Sutton*, *Gre-*

sham, *Craven* and *Spencer*; so that he must be naturally Blind, or put out his Eyes, who doth not see that the **Abatement of Interest is a Diffusive Principle**: Hence it follows, that as few Great and Rich Merchants, whose Estates are Personal (except they have also great Souls) can bear the Discourse of Abating Interest with more Patience than Usurers, well knowing that it must necessarily retrench their present Profits by encreasing the number of Traders; which though it be a small loss to Individuals, will be a vast gain to the generality of the Nation. At the lower end of Page 12. His Words are, that in my instance of old *Audley*'s observing that 100 *l.* at 10 *per cent*, would in 70 Years amount to 100000 *l.* he affirms, *I am no less mistaken than in other things*.

Truly, if I have mistook no more in other things than in that, in such an untroden Path as this I have failed much less than I could hope for; to demonstrate which I have here inserted a short Table, shewing that 100 *l.* at that Rate, riseth (within a trifle) to 200 *l.* in Seven Years, Interest upon Interest; so that the usual Accompt is and was formerly, that Money doubles once in Seven Years, at 10 *per cent*, according to which Rule 100 *l.* in Seventy Years, amounts to 102400 *l.*

One

One Hundred Pounds at Ten Pounds per Cent, per Annum, *at Interest upon Interest, encreaseth thus,* viz.

	L.	S.	D.
AT first,	100	00	00
At 3 Months, it is	102	10	00
At 6 Months,	105	1	03
At 9 Months,	107	13	9
At 12 Months,	110	07	7
At 1 Year $\frac{1}{4}$	113	02	9
At 1 Year $\frac{1}{2}$	115	19	4
At 1 Year $\frac{3}{4}$	118	17	4
At 2 Years,	121	16	9
At 2 Years $\frac{1}{4}$	124	17	8
At 2 Years $\frac{1}{2}$	128	00	1
At 2 Years $\frac{3}{4}$	131	4	1
At 3 Years,	134	9	9
At 3 Years $\frac{1}{4}$	137	17	0
At 3 Years $\frac{1}{2}$	141	5	10
At 3 Years $\frac{3}{4}$	144	16	6
At 4 Years,	148	8	11
At 4 Years $\frac{1}{4}$	152	3	1
At 4 Years $\frac{1}{2}$	155	19	2
At 4 Years $\frac{3}{4}$	159	17	2
At 5 Years,	163	17	1
At 5 Years $\frac{1}{4}$	167	19	0
At 5 Years $\frac{1}{2}$	172	3	0
At 5 Years $\frac{3}{4}$	176	9	1
At 6 Years,	180	17	3

At 6 Years ¼	185	7	9
At 6 Years ½	190	5	0
At 6 Years ¾	194	15	5
At 7 Years,	199	12	10

Supposing One Hundred Pounds to double in Seven Years at Interest upon Interest, as aforesaid, the encrease is, viz.

	L.
At first	100
At 7 Years	200
At 14 Years	400
At 21 Years	800
At 28 Years	1600
At 35 Years	3200
At 42 Years	6400
At 49 Years	12800
At 56 Years	25600
At 63 Years	51200
At 70 Years	102400

Page 13. he saith, *That I make use of the Abuse of Interest, which no Man pleads for, annexing a Discourse against Interest, writ in* 1621. *when it was at* 13 per cent, *endeavouring thereby to impose a Belief that the Gentleman who writ that Discourse was of my mind; whereas it may be supposed, the Author of that Book was contented with* 8 per cent, *because within Four Years after it was brought down to that Rate, and that other-*

otherwise he would have writ further, it being probable that he might live till after Four Years.

I answer, That through the Mercies of Almighty God, and for the Good of this Kingdom, that Patriot of his Country, Old Sir *Thomas Culpepper*, who I have since been assured was the Author of that Treatise, did live above Twenty Years after the writing thereof; and then published a Second Treatise, which was lately Re-printed by his worthy Son; which Second Treatise is now to be had at Mr. *Wilkinson*'s, over against St. *Dunstan*'s Church in *Fleet-Street*, which I would advise my Opposer to Read, and then I hope he will be more modest hereafter, than to mis-call the most Natural and Rational Conclusions, *IMPOSINGS*.

But lest he should not meet with the said Treatise, I shall here insert a few Lines out of it to the present purpose, *viz.*

Old Sir *Thomas* speaking of the certain good Effects of the Abatement of Interest from 10 to 8 *per cent*, Page 19. of his Second Treatise, saith, *This good success doth call upon us not to rest here, but that we bring the Use for Money to a lower Rate, which now I suppose will find no Opposition; for all Objections, which before the Statute were made against it, are now answered by the Success; and most certainly the benefit will be much greater to the Common Wealth, by*

calling

calling the Use for Money down from 8 *to* 5 *or* 6 per cent, *than it was from calling it down from* 10 *to* 8 per cent. I ſhall not Comment upon his Words, but only declare that, in Truth, I never heard of this Treatiſe, nor of any other to the like effect, when I wrote mine.

Page 13. The Gentleman brings up his Batalia, and, like a ſtout Champion for the ſlie and timorous heard of Uſurers, plants his main Battery againſt that part which I confeſſed to be weakeſt, *viz.* that the difficulty of this Queſtion is, *Whether the lowneſs of Intereſt be the cauſe or the Effect of Riches?* And he poſitively denies that the lowneſs of Intereſt is the Cauſe, and affirms it to be only the Effect thereof; which he endeavours to prove by four Arguments, which I ſhall particularly Anſwer in due place; in the mean time uſe my own method to prove, *That the Abatement of Intereſt by a Law in* England *will be a means to improve the Riches of this Kingdom:* And I prove it thus;

What-

Whatever doth

1. Advance the value of Land in Purchase,
2. Improve the Rent of Farms,
3. Encrease the bulk of Foreign Trade,
4. Multiply domestick Artificers,
5. Encline the Nation to Thriftiness,
6. Employ the Poor,
7. Encrease the Stock of People,

Must be a procuring cause of Riches.

Now, that the Abatement of Interest will advance the value of Land, I prove first by Experience, for certainly *Anno* 1621. the currant

currant Price of our Lands in *England*, was Twelve Years Purchase: And so I have been assured by many Ancient Men whom I have queried particularly as to this Matter; and I find it so by purchases made about that time by my own Relations and Acquaintance; and I presume that any Nobleman or Gentleman of *England*, by only commanding the Stewards of their Mannors to give them Lists out of Records of any Mannors and Farms that their Grand-Fathers, or Fathers, bought or sold Fifty Years past, will find that the same Farms, to be now Sold, would yield (one with another) at least treble the Money, and in some cases six times the Money they were then Bought and Sold for; which I submit still to the single and joint Judgments of the Honourable Members of both Houses of Parliament; who, being the greatest Owners of our Territory, are, in their private, as well as in their Politick, Capacities, the most proper and experimental Judges of this Case; if the Ancient of them will please to recollect their Memories, and the Younger will please to be informed by their Elder Servants; and if this be so, it cannot be denied, but the Abatement of Interest by a Law, hath greatly advanced Lands in Purchase as well as improved Rents, by meliorating the

Lands

Lands themſelves, thoſe improvements by Marling, Limeing, Draining, &c. having been made ſince Money was at 8 and 6 *per cent*, which 10 *per cent* could not bear.

And to prove that Lands were then at Twelve Years Purchaſe, I have the written Teſtimony of that incomparable worthy Perſon Sir *Thomas Culpepper*, Senior, who, Page 11. of his firſt Treatiſe, expreſly affirms, *That Land was then at Twelve Years Purchaſe*; who, being himſelf a Grave and Ancient Parliament Man, and dedicating his Book to the then Parliament, whereof he was then a Member, cannot, without horrible Uncharitableneſs, be preſumed to impoſe upon his Country.

And now that our Intereſt is at 6 *per cent*, as the ſame worthy Author did wiſely foreſee, I appeal to the Judgment and Experience of my Country-Men, whether the genuine Price of our Lands in *England* now would not be 20 Years Purchaſe, were it not for accidental Preſſures, under which it labours at preſent, ſuch as theſe;

1. Our late great Land-Taxes.

2. And principally the late great improvement of *Ireland*, mentioned in my former Treatiſe, the conſequence whereof is, that that Country now ſupplieth Foreign Markets, as well as our own Plantations

in

in *America*, with Beef, Pork, Hides, Tallow, Bread, Beer, Wool and Corn, at cheaper Rates than we can afford, to the beating us out of those Trades; whereas formerly, *viz*. Presently after the late *Irish* War, many Men got good Estates by Transporting *English* Cattle thither.

And that the Improvement of *Ireland*, is the principal cause why our Lands in Purchase rise not as naturally they should, with the fall of our Interest, appears evidently from the effect the fall of Interest hath had upon Houses in *London*; where the growth of *Ireland* could have no such destructive Influence; which hath been so considerable, that whosoever will please to inform themselves by old Scriveners, or ancient Deeds, shall find, that a House in *London*, about Fifty Years past, that would sell but for 300 *l*. at most, would readily sell within a short time after Interest was brought to 8 *per cent*, at 5 or 600 *l*. and the same Houses to be sold sometime after Interest was brought to 6 *per cent*, *viz*. before and after the late *Dutch* War, would have yielded without scruple 1000 or 1200 *l*. The Abatement of Interest having had a double effect upon Houses, by encreasing Trade, and consequently raising Rents, as well as encreasing the number of Years Purchase.

3. A third Reason why Land doth not at present bear an exact Proportion to 6 *per cent*, which should naturally be twenty Years, is the late Plague which did much depopulate this Kingdom.

4. The late Fire in *London*, which hath engaged Men in Building in the City, who otherwise would have been Purchasing in the Country.

5. The usual Plenty of Corn, which hath been for these three or four Years past in most parts of *Christendom*, the like whereof hath been seldom known, it happening most commonly, that when one Country hath had great Plenty, others have had great Scarcity.

6. *The racking up of Rents in the Year* 1651. and 1653. which was presently after the last Abatement of *Interest*.

A Seventh accidental Reason why Land doth not Sell at present, at the Rate it naturally should, in proportion to the legal Interest, is, *That innovated Practice of Bankers in* London, which hath more effects attending it than most I converse with have yet observed; but I shall here take notice of that only which is to my present purpose, *viz.*

The *Gentlemen*, that are *Bankers*, having a large Interest from his *Majesty*, for what they advance upon his *Majesties Revenue*; can afford

afford to give the full legal Interest to all Persons that put Money into their Hands, though for never so short or long a time; which makes the Trade of Usury so easie, and hitherto safe, that few, after having found the sweetness of this lasie way of improvement (being by continuance and success grown to fancy themselves secure in it) can be led (there being neither ease nor profit to invite them) to lay out their Money in Land, though at 15 Years Purchase; whereas before this way of private Bankering came up, Men that had Money were forced oftentimes to let it lye dead by them, until they could meet with Securities to their minds; and if the like necessity were now of Money lying dead, the loss of Use for the dead time being deducted from the profit of 6 *l. per cent (communibus annis)* would in effect take off 1 *l. per cent per annum* of the profit of Usury, and consequently incline Men more to Purchase Lands, in regard the difference between Usury and Purchasing would not in point of profit be so great as now it is; this new Invention of Cashiering, having in my opinion clearly bettered the Usurers Trade 1 or 2 *per cent per annum*. And that this way of leaving Money with *Gold-Smiths* hath had the aforesaid effect, seems evident to me from the Scarcity it makes

makes of Money in the Country; for the Trade of *Bankers* being only in *London*, doth very much drain the ready Money from all other parts of the Kingdom.

The ſecond point I am to prove, is, That it will advance the Rent of Farms.

To prove that it did ſo in fact, depends on memory; and for my own part, I, and moſt others I converſe with, do perfectly remember that Rents did generally riſe after the late abatement of Intereſt, (*viz.*) in the year 1651. and 1652.

The reaſon why they did ſo, was from the encouragement which that abatement of Intereſt gave to *Landlords* and *Tenants*, to improve by *Draining*, *Marling*, *Limeing*, &c. excellently made out by the aforeſaid two worthy Authors, ſo that I do (I think with good Reaſon) conclude that the preſent fall of Rents is not natural, but accidental, and to be aſcribed principally to the foregoing Reaſons, given for the preſent abatement of Land in purchaſe, and eſpecially to the late Improvement of *Ireland*.

The third thing I am to prove, is, That the abatement of Intereſt will encreaſe the bulk of foreign Trade, which I do thus.

By evidence of fact, it hath been ſo in *England, the encreaſe of our Trade hath always followed the abatement of our Intereſt by Law*, I ſay, not preceded, but followed it, and the Cause doth always go before the effect, which I think I have evidently demonstrated in my former Treatise.

If any doubt of this, and will be at the pains to examin the *Custom-house* Books, they may soon be resolved.

2. *By Authority*; not only of that ancient *Gentleman Sir Thomas Culpepper* in his second Treatise, and therein of the Judgement of the *French King* and Court, in an *Edict* there recited; but likewise of a *Parliament of England, King, Lords and Commons*, in the *Act* for reducing it to 6 *per cent*, in the preamble whereof are these Words, *viz. Forasmuch as the Abatement of Interest from* 10 *in the Hundred in former times, hath been found by notable Experience beneficial to the Advancement of Trade, and improvement of Lands by good Husbandry, with many other considerable Advantages to this Nation, especially the reducing of it to a nearer proportion with foreign States, with whom we traffick: And whereas in fresh memory the like fall from* 8 *to* 6 *in the Hundred by a late constant Practice, hath found the like success to the general contentment of this Nation, as is visible by several Improvements, &c.*

3. *By necessary consequences*; when Interest is abated, they who call in their Money must either buy Land or Trade with it: If they

bu

buy Land the many Buyers will raise th price of Land: If they Trade they encrea the number of Traders, and consequent the bulk of Trade; and let their Money lie dead by them, I think I have fully proved they cannot, in an addition I publish to my first *Observations.*

4. *By reason*; for first, whilst Interest is at 6 *per cent*, no Man will run an adventure to Sea for the gain of 8 or 9 *per cent*, which the *Dutch* having Money at 4 or 3 *per cent* at Interest are contented with, and therefore can and do follow a vast trade in Salt from St. *Vual*, *Rochel*, and other parts of the *Baltick Seas*, and also their *fishing Trade* for *Herrings* and *Whale-fishing*, which we neglect, as being not worth our trouble and hazard, while we can make 6 *per cent* of our Money sleeping. For the measure of our Money employed in Trade in any Nation, bears an exact proportion to the Interest paid for Money; as for instance, when Money was at 10 *per cent* in *England*, no man in his wits would follow any Trade whereby he did not promise himself 14 or 12 *per cent* again at least; when Interest was at 8, the hopes of 12 or 10 at least was necessary; as 8 or 9 *per cent* is, now Interest goes at 6 *per cent*; the infallible Consequnce whereof is, that the Trades before recited, as well as those of

Muscovy and *Greenland*, and so much at lea[st] of all others, that will not afford us a clea[r] profit of 8 or 9 *per cent*, we carelesly giv[e] away to the *Dutch*, and must do so for ever unless we bring our Interest nearer to a *Pa[rity]* with theirs; and hence in my poor Opini[on] it follows very clearly, that if our Inte[rest] were abated one third part, it woul[d] occasion the employment of one third pa[rt] more of Men, Shipping and Stock, in for[eign] and domestick Trades.

This discovers the vanity of all our At[tempts] for gaining of the *White-Herring Fishing-Trade*, of which the *Dutch*, as every body observes, make wonderful great advan[tage], though the Fish be taken upon our own *Coasts*; I wish as many did take notice of th[e] Reason of it, which therefore I shall say some[thing] of now, though I have touched it [in] my former Treatise.

The plain case is this, *A Dutch-man* w[ill] be content to employ a Stock of 5 or 1000 *l* in *Burses*, *Materials for fishing*, *Victuals*, &[c.] for the carrying on of this Trade; and if [at] the winding up of his Accounts, he finds [he] hath got clear, *communibus annis*, for h[is] Stock and Adventure 5 *per cent per annum*, [he] thanks God and tels his neighbours he ha[th] had a thriving Trade: Now while eve[ry] slothful ignorant Man with us, that hath b[...]

wit enough to tell out his Money to a *Goldsmith*, can get 6 *per cent* without pains or care; is it not monstrous absurd to imagine that ever the *English* will do any good upon this Trade, till they begin an the right end, which must be to reduce the Interest of Money?

Secondly, The depraved nature of Man affecting ease and pleasure, while use of Money runs at 6 *per cent*, hath always at hand an easie expedient to indulge that humor, and reconcile it to another as considerable, viz. his Covetousness, by putting his Money to use; and if a *Merchant* through his youthful care and industry, arrive to an Estate of 20000 *l.* in twenty Years trading, whilst Money is so high, and Land so low, he can easily turn Country *Gentleman* or Usurer; which, were Interest of Money at 4 per cent, he could not do; and consequently must not only follow his Trade himself, but make his Children Traders also; for to leave them Money without skill to use it, would advantage little; and purchasing of Lands less, when the fall of Interest shall raise them to twenty or thirty Years purchase, which I hope yet to live to see.

Thirdly, From this necessity of *Merchants* keeping to their Trade, and *Childrens* succeeding their Fathers therein, would ensue to *Merchants* greater skill in Trade, more exact and certain correſpondency, ſurer and more truſty *Factors* abroad, and thoſe better acquainted and concatenated together by the experimental Links of each others Humors, Stile, Eſtate and Buſineſs. And whereas it is as much as a prudent Man can do in ten years time, after his ſettling in *London*, to be exactly well fitted with *Factors* in all parts, and thoſe by correſpondency brought into a mutual Acquaintance of each other, and honeſt *Work-men* and *Maſters* of Ships, &c. And by that time he hath traded ten Years longer, if he ſucceed well, it is ſix to one but he leaves Trade, and turns *Country-Gentleman*, or *Uſurer*, and ſo that profitable Engine (the Wheels whereof by Correſpondency move one another in many parts of the World) which he hath been ſo long a framing, within a few Years after it is brought to work well, is broken to pieces, and the benefit thereof to the Kingdom (which is ten times more than to him that made it) is loſt, whereas in *Holland* and *Italy*, where Money is at 3 or 4 *per cent*, and conſequently *Merchants* forc'd to keep and truſt to their Trades only, their Buſineſſes are, and muſt be ſo ordered and carried on from the beginning, that when a Man die, the Tr e

is

is no more disturb'd than when the Wife dies in *England.*

I am ashamed of the odious Prolixity and Repetition I am (contrary to my Nature) forced to use ; but my *Opposer* doth so often, and I think disingenuously, upbraid me with begging the Question, that I am compelled to it.

The *fourth* thing I am to prove, is, that *It multiplies Domestick Artificers.*

If the former be true, that it encreases foreign Trade, I suppose no Man will have the confidence to deny this to be a necessary and infallible consequence of that : For we see througout the World, where ever there is the greatest Trade, there are the most *Artificers* ; and that since our own Trade encreased in *England*, our *Artificers* of all sorts are proportionably encreased. The building of *London* hath made multitudes of *Bricklayers* and *Carpenters* ; much use of *Shipping* will make Ships dear, and the dearness of Shipping will make many *Shipwrights* ; much *foreign Trade*, will encrease the vent of our *Native Manufactures*, and much vent will make many work-men ; and if we cannot get and breed them fast enough our selves, we shall draw them from foreign parts, as the *Dutch* draw away ours ; it being a wise and true observation of (as I remember) Sir *Walter Rawleigh*, **That no Nation can want People that hath good Laws.**

The *fifth* thing to be proved, is, that *It enclines a Nation to thriftiness*; this is likewise consequent to the former, and by experience made good in *England*; for since our Trade encreased, tho' the generality of our Nation are grown richer, as I have shewed, and consequently more splendid in Cloaths, Plate, Jewels, Houshold-stuff, and all other outward signs of Riches; yet are we not half so much given to Hospitality and good House-keeping (as it is called) as in former days, when our greatest expence was upon our Bellies, the most destructive Consumption that can happen to a Nation, and tending only to nourish Idleness, Luxury, and Beggary; whereas that other kind of Expence which follows Trade, encourageth Labour, Arts and Invention: To which give me leave to add, that *The abatement of Interest conjoyn'd with Excises upon our home consumption* (if the latter could be hit upon without disturbance to Trade, or danger of continuation) *are two of the most comprehensive and effectual* **Sumptuary Laws**, *that ever were established in any Nation*, and most necessitating and engaging any People to thriftiness, the high Road to Riches, as well for Nations as private Families.

The

The frugal *Italians* of Old, and the provident *Dutch* of later times, I think, I have given the World a ſufficient proof of this *Theorem:* And if any ſhall tell me, it is the nature of thoſe People to be thrifty; I anſwer, all Men by nature are alike; it is only Laws, Cuſtoms, and Education that differ Men; *their Nature and Diſpoſition, and the diſpoſition of all People in the World, proceed from their Laws*; the *French Peaſantry* are a ſlaviſh, cowardly People, becauſe the Laws of their Country have made them Slaves; the *French Gentry*, a noble, valiant People, becauſe free by Law, Birth and Education: In *England* we are all free Subjects by our Laws, and therefore our People prove generally couragious; the *Dutch* and *Italians* are both frugal Nations, though their Climates and Governments differ as much as any, becauſe the Laws of both Nations encline them to Thriftineſs; other Nations I could name, are generally vain and prodigal not by Nature, nor for want of a good Country; but becauſe their Laws, *&c.* diſpoſe them ſo to be.

The *ſixth* proof of the *Propoſition*, is, that *it employs the Poor*; which is a neceſſary Conſequence likewiſe of the encreaſe of Trade in *Cities*, and Emprovement of Land in the *Country*; which is well and truly demonſtrated ed from experience, by the Elder and Younger Sir *Thomas Culpepper*, to whom, to avoid Proxility, I must refer the Reader.

Seventhly, It encreaseth the People of a Nation; this also necessarily followeth the encrease of Trade and Improvement of Lands, not that it causeth married Men to get more Children.

But 1*st*, a trading Country affording comfortable Subsistances to more Families than a Country distitute of Trade, is the reason that many do Marry, who othehwise must be forced to live single; which may be one reason why fewer People of either Sex are to be seen unmarried in *Holland* at 25 years of age, than may be found in *England* at 40 years old.

2*dly*, Where there is much Employment, and good Pay, if we want Hands of our own we shall draw them from others, as hath been said.

3*dly*, We shall keep our own People at home, which otherwise for want of Employment would be forced to leave us, and serve other Nations, as too many of our Sea-men, Shipwrights, and others have done.

4*thly*, Our Lands and Trade being improved, will render us capable not only of employing, but feeding a far greater number of People, as is manifest in that instance of the Land of *Palestine*. And

And if these will be the effects of abating Interest, then I think it is out of doubt that the Abatement of Interest is the cause of the encrease of the Riches of any Kingdom, for *quicquid efficit tale est magis tale.* Now to answer his four recited Reasons, *viz.*

First, he saith, *If a low stated Interest by Law be the cause of Riches, no Country would be poor*, all desiring Riches rather than Poverty, and all having it in their Power to state their Interest as low as they please by Law.

I answer, *first*, *Whatever Nation doth it gradually*, for so it must be done, as it hath been hitherto in *England* (2 *per cent* being enough to abate at one time) *will find those effects I have mentioned*; but it is a work of Ages, and cannot be done at once; For **Nec natura aut lex operantur per saltum.**

Secondly, It is great Imprudence to imagine that any Country understanding their true Interest so well, as by degrees to abate Use-money, will not likewise by the same Wisdom be led to the instituting of many other good Laws for the encouragement of Trade, as our *Parliament* have still proceeded to do, as Interest hath been abated.

His *second* Reason is, *That if the lowness of Interest were not the effect of Riches in* Holland, *they*

they might take as much Use-Money as they could get, there being no Law against it.

I answer, There were formerly Laws in *Holland* that reduced Interest to 8 and 6, and afterwards to 5 *per cent*, *Anno* 1640. and since in the Year 1655. to 4 *per cent*, the *Placart* for which I have seen, and have been told, and do believe they have since reduced it by *Placart* to 3 *per cent*, as to their *Cantors*, and all publick Receipts; which in *Holland* is as much in effect as if they had made a general Law for it, because the most of their Receipts and Payments are made in and out of the aforesaid publick Offices, or else into and out of their Banks, for which no Use-Money is allowed; which several gradual and successful abatements of Interest did occasion their Riches at first, and brought their People to that Consistency of Wealth, that they have since wrought themselves into such an abundance, that *there are more lenders now than Borrowers*, and so I doubt not but it will be with us in a few Years, after the next abatement of *Interest* is made by Law; which I have good reason to conclude, not only from the visible operations of nature in all other things and places, but from Fact and Experience in this very case; being certain that the *Gold-Smiths* in *London* could have what money they would upon their Servants Notes only, at 4 *l.* 10 *s. per cent*, before the late Emergencies of State; which I could demonſtrate have very much obſtructed the natural fall of Intereſt with us; ſomething more I have ſaid in anſwer to this in the addition to my former Treatiſe; and this may ſerve likewiſe for an anſwer to his third Reaſon.

Fourthly, he ſaith, *That which I muſt prove to make good my Aſſertion, is. that any Country in the World from a poor and low condition, while Intereſt was at 6* per cent, *was made Rich by bringing it to 4* per cent, *or* 3 per cent *by a Law.*

I anſwer, If the inſtance of *Holland* and *Italy* were not ſufficient to ſatisfie him in this point, yea that having proved (which he cannot deny) that our own *Kingdom* hath been enriched conſequently, conſtantly and proportionably to and after our ſeveral abatements of Intereſt by Law, from an unlimited rate, to 10, from 10 to 8, and from 8 to 6 *per cent*, I think it may rationally be concluded that another Abatement of Intereſt in *England* would cauſe a further encreaſe of Riches, as it hath done in *Holland.*

From *Italy* I have endeavoured to gain a certain account of their *Legal Intereſt*, but am adviſed that no taking of Uſe-Money is allowed by their *Pontifical Laws*; the Intereſt

now

now taken there, which is generally 4 *per cent*, is done only by dispensation of Pope *Paul* the *fifth*, and that notwithstanding *no Man can recover Interest of Money there, if the party who should pay it can prove he hath not gained the value of the Interest demanded:* Now let the Reader judge whether that practice of *Holland* and this of *Italy*, where the *Romish-Church-men* have so great Power, who are to take Cognizance, and may by their Auricular *Confessions*, of all Offences of this kind, the Laws concerning the use of Money in those Countries being *Pontifical*, do not amount in effect to a low stated Interest by Law in *England*.

But to deal more ingenuously with my *Opposer* than he hath done with me, I will grant him that much Riches will occasion in any Kingdom a low rate of Interest, and yet that doth not hinder but a low stated Interest by Law may be a cause of Riches: For if Trade be that which enricheth any Kingdom, and lowering of Interest advanceth Trade (which I think is sufficiently proved) then the Abatement of Interest, or more properly restraining of Usury; which the ancient *Romans*, and all other Wise and Rich People in the world did always drive at; is doubtless a primary and principal cause of the Riches of any *Nation*; it being not improper

proper to ſay, not abſurd to conceive, that *The ſame thing may be both a Cauſe and an Effect.* Peace begets Plenty, and Plenty may be a means to preſerve Peace: Fear begets Hatred, and Hatred Fear: The diligent hand makes Rich, anh Riches makes Men diligent, ſo true is the Proverb, *Creſcit amor Nummi, quantum ipſa pecunia creſcit*; Love we ſay begets Love, the fertility of a Country may cauſe the encreaſe of People, and the encreaſe of People may cauſe the further and greater fertility of a Country; Liberty and Property conduce to the encreaſe of Trade and Emprovement of any Country, and the encreaſe of Trade and Emprovements conduce to the procuring, as well as ſecuring, of Liberty and Property; Strength and Health conduce to a good digeſtion, and a good digeſtion is neceſſary to the preſervation of Health & encreaſe of Strength; and as a perſon of very great honour pertinently inſtanced at a late debate upon this Queſtion, *An Egg is the cauſe of a Hen, and a Hen the cauſe of an Egg.* The incomparable *Lord Bacon* in his Hiſtory of *Henry* the 7th. ſaith, page 245. of that *Prince* as well as other Men: That his Fortune worked upon his Nature, and his Nature upon his Fortune; the like may be ſaid of Nations; *The abatement of Intereſt cauſeth an encreaſe of*

Wealth

Wealth, and the encrease of Wealth may cause a further abatement of Interest. But that is best done by the Midwifery of good Laws, which is what I plead for; the corrupt Nature of Man being more apt to decline to Vice, than incline to Vertue.

Folio 15. he affirms, *Lands are not risen in purchase, nor rents improved, since the Abatement of Interest.*

That I shall say no more to; it is matter of Fact, and *Gentlemen* who are the *owners* of Land are the best Judges of this case; only I would entreat them not to depend upon their Memories alone, but to command particular accompts to be given them what sum or sums of Money were given 40 or 50 years past for any entire Farms or Mannors they now know; and I doubt not but they will find that most of them will yield double the said sums of Money now, notwithstanding the present great pressures that Land lies under, which ought maturely to be considered of: when this Judgment is made, I rather desire the enquiry to be made upon the gross sum of Money paid, than the years Purchase, as being less fallible; because many Farms have been of late years so rackt up in Rents, that it may be they will not yield more years purchase now, according to the present Rents, than they would many years past, and yet may yield double the

Mo-

Money they were then Bought or Sold for, becauſe the Rents were much leſs then.

Fol. 15. He Impertinently Quarrels at my Inſtance of *Ireland*, ſaying, I quote it ſometimes to prove the benefit of a low Intereſt, Pag. 8. And ſometimes the miſchief of high Intereſt, Page 9. Which ſeems to me to be an unfriendly way of Prevaricating: For Page 8. I mention the late great Improvement of *Ireland* only, as an accidental Cauſe why our Rents at that preſent fell; and in this it appears I was not much miſtaken, for within a few Months after I firſt writ that Treatiſe, the *Parliament* took notice of it. Page 9. I mention that place among others, that pay a high Intereſt, and are conſequently very Poor: If there be any Contradiction in this, let the Reader judge. Page 16. the *Gentleman* puzles himſelf about finding Miſtakes in my Calculation of the encreaſe of *Merchants* Eſtates, but diſcovers none but his own; ſo I ſhall not trouble the Reader further about that, all *Merchants* granting me as much as I deſign by it; tho' ſome of them have not, or care not to obſerve the Abatement of Intereſt to have been the principal Cauſe thereof.

Fol. 17. Becauſe he cannot anſwer that large and Pregnant Inſtance of the effects of low Intereſt which I gave, in the caſe of

H the

the *Sugar-Bakers* of *London*, and those of *Holland*, which was but one of a Hundred which I could have mentioned; he endeavours to set up another of a contrary effect, which is a weak ridiculous Instance, and nothing to his purpose; for that Commodity that I mentioned, *viz. Sugar*, is a solid bulky Commodity, always in fashion, not consequent to Humour, as is that of *Silk-Stockings*, 1000 *l* worth whereof may be with less Charge carried to *Italy*, than 30 *l.* worth of *Barbadoes Sugar* can be sent to *Holland*: Besides, the reason why we of late sent Silk-Stockings thither, is accidental, not natural, only happening by means of an Engine we have to Weave them, whereof they have not yet the use in *Italy*: Besides, wearing things being more esteemed through Fancy than Judgment, the *Italians* may have the same variety which is too much amongst us, to esteem that which is none of their own making, as we do *French Ribonds*, and the *French-men English* ones; besides, he is mistaken in saying, We bring the Silk we make them of from *Italy*, for the Silk of which we make that Commodity is *Turkey*, not *Italian*, Silk.

Fol. 18. The *Gentleman* begins to be kind and finding me out of the way, pretends to set me right, *viz.* to Instruct me, as first what will bring down *Interest*.

1st, *Multitude of People.*

2dly, *A full Trade.*

3dly, *Liberty of Conscience.*

I Answer; That I have, I think, proved, that the Abatement of Interest will effect the two former; and I think my *Opposer* is not clear sighted, if he cannot discern that the latter, in a due and regulated Proportion, must be a consequent of them.

In the next place, the *Gentleman* finding me at a loss, as he says, for the Reason of our great Trade at present, will help me as well as he can.

I answer; Those latter Words (*as well as he can*) were well put in, for as yet he hath told me no news, nor given any shadow of Reason that I knew not before, and had maturely considered on many Years before I writ the first Tratise.

The Reasons he gives for our present greatness of Trade are;

First, *Our casting off the Church of* Rome.

Secondly, *The Statutes in* Henry *the 7th's time prohibiting Noble-mens Retainers, and making their Lands liable to the Payment of Debts.*

Thirdly, *The Discovery of the* East *and* West-India *Trades*, p. 19, 20.

To his first and second Reasons, I answer, *That those Statutes of* Henry *the 7th, and our casting off the Church of* Rome *did long precede our being any thing in Trade*; which began not until the latter end of Queen *Elizabeth's* Reign, and afterwards encreased in the time of King *James* and King *Charles* the first, as we Abated our Interest, and not otherwise; *there being a Person yet living*, and but 77 Years of Age, *viz.* Captain *Russel* of *Wapping*, *Who assures me, he can remember since we had not above three Merchants Ships of* 300 *Tuns, and upwards, belonging to* England.

Secondly, That in *Italy*, where there are no such Statutes for Abridgement of *Noblemen's* Retainers, nor casting off the *Church* of *Rome*, there is notwithstanding a very great Trade, and Land at from 35 to 40 Years Purchase, which sufficiently shews that a low Interest is absolutely and principally necessary, and that the other particulars alone will not do, to the procuring of those ends, although a low Interest singly doth it in *Italy*.

To his third Reason, I answer, that *There are some Men yet living who, do remember a greater Trade to* East-India, *and a far greater Stock employed therein, than we have now*; and yet we were so far from thriving upon it, that we lost by it, and could never see our Principal Money again; Nor ever did we greatly Prosper upon it, till our Interest was much Abated by Laws; *nor ever shall match*

th

the Dutch *in it, till our Interest be as low as theirs.* The like, in a great measure, is true in our *West-India* Trades, we never got considerable by them till our last Abatement of Interest from 8 to 6 *per cent.*

Page 21, 22. he labours to prove, That *if we would have Trade to flourish, and Lands high, we must imitate the* Hollanders *in their Practices*; which in matter of Trade I know is most certain. so far as they are consistent with the Government of our own Country: And the first and readiest thing wherein we can imitate them, is to reduce our Interest of Money to a lower Rate, after the manner of our Fathers, & as they did it before us, which will naturally lead us to all the other advantages in Trade which they now use.

1. For, *If Interest be Abated to* 4 per cent *who will not, that can leave his Children any competent Estate of* 1000 *or* 2000 *l. each, bring them up to Writings, Arithmetick, and Merchants Accompts, and instruct them in Trades,* well knowing that the bare Use of their Money, or the product of it in Land, will scarce keep them?

2. *Must not all Persons live lower in Expence, when all Trades will be less gainful to Individuals, though more profitable to the Publick?*

3. *Will it not put us upon Building as bulky and cheap Sailing Ships as they?*

4. *Will it not bring Trade to be so familiar amongst us, that our Gentlemen,* who are in our greatest *Councils, will come to understand it, and accordingly contrive Laws in favour of it?*

5. *Will it not; nay, hath it not, already brought us to lower our Customs upon our own Native Commodities and Manufactures.*

6. *Will it not in time bring us to transferring Bills of Debt?* Is not necessity the Mother of Invention, and that old Proverb true, **Facile est inventis addere**? There is in my poor Opinion nothing conduceable to the good of Trade, that we shall not by one accident or other hit upon, when we have attained this Fundamental Point, and are thereby necessitated to follow and keep to our Trades from Generation to Generation.

7. Do we not see that even as the World now goes, **Dies diem docet**? scarce a Sessions of *Parliament* passeth without making some good Acts for the bettering of Trade and pareing of the extravagancy of the Law; for which ends this last Session produced three.

That about the Silk-Throwsters.

That about Transportation of Hedes, &c.

That about Writs of Error.

8. *Will not the full understanding of Trade* (acquired by Experience, and never wanting to any People that make it their constant busine

business to follow Trade, as we must do when Interest shall be at 4 *per cent*) *quickly bring us to find our advantage in permitting all Strangers to co-habit, Trade and Purchase Lands amongst us upon as easie Terms as the* Dutch *do?*

Will not the Consequence of this Law, by augmenting the value of Land, *bring us in time to regular and just Enclosements of our Forrests, Commons and Wastes, and making our smaller Rivers Navigable?* The highest Improvements that this Land is capable of: And have not these last 50 Years, since the several Abatement of Interest, produced more of these profitable Works than 200 Years before?

Will not the Consequence of this Law discover to us the vanity and opposition to Trade that there seems to be in many of our Statutes yet in force, such as these following, *viz.*

1st, *The Statutes of Bankrupt* (as they are now used) *in many Cases more to the prejudice of honest Dealers than the Bankrupt himself*, by compelling Men often times to refund Money received of the *Bankrupt* for Wares justly sold and delivered him, long before it was possible for the *Seller* to discover the *Buyer* to be a *Bankrupt*.

2dly, *Such are our Laws limiting the price of Beer and Ale to one Penny* per *Quart*, which bar us from all Improvements and Imitation of Foreign Liquors made of Corn, commonly celled *Mum*, *Spruce-Beer*, *Rostcker-Beer*, which may, and are made in *England*, and would occasion the profitable Consumption of an incredible quantity of our Grain, and prove a great addition to His Majesties Revenue of Excise, expend abundance of *Coals* in long boyling of those Commodities, imploy many Hands in the Manufacture of them, as well as Shipping in Transportation of them, not only to all our own Plantations in *America*, but to many other parts of the World.

3dly, *Our Laws against engrossing Corn and other Commodities*, There being no Persons more beneficial to a Trade in a *Nation*, than *Engrossers*, which will be a worthy Employment for our present *Usurers*, and render them truly useful to their Country.

4thly, *Such was our Law against Exportation of Bullion lately repealed.*

5thly, *Such is the use of the Law at present, which takes not only a Custom, but* 15 s. per *Tun Excise on Strong Beer exported*, being the same Rate it pays when spent at home, contrary to the Practice of all Trading *Countries*.

6thly, *Such are our Laws which charge Sea-Coals, or any of our Native Provisions exported, with Custom*, viz. Beef, Pork, Bread, Beer, *&c.* For which I think in prudence the

Door

Door ſhould be opened wide to let them out.

7thly, *Of the like nature is our Law impoſing a great Duty upon our Horſes, Mares, and Nags exported.*

8thly, *Such, in my weak opinion, is that branch of the Statute of 5* Eliz. *that none ſhould uſe any Manual Occupation except he hath been Apprentice to the ſame.*

9thly, *Such* (in my Opinion) *is the Law which yet prohibits the Exportation of our own Coin*; for ſince it is now by conſent of Parliament agreed and found by Experience of all Underſtanding Men, to be advantagious for this Kingdom to permit the free exportation of *Bullion*, I think it were better for us that our own Coin might likewiſe be freely exported, becauſe by what of that went out we ſhould gain the Manufacture (the Coyning) beſides the great honour and note of Magnificency it would be to His *Majeſty* and this Kingdom, to have His *Majeſties Coin* currant in all parts of the *Univerſe.*

10thy, *Such are all By-laws uſed among the Society of Coopers, and other Artificers, limiting Maſters to keep but one Apprentice at a time*; whereas it were better for the publick, they were permitted to keep Ten, if they could or would maintain or employ them.

11thly, *Such ſeem to be many of our Laws relating to the Poor, eſpecially thoſe againſt Inmates*

mates in Cities and Trading Towns, and those obliging Parishes to maintain their own Poor only.

Page 23. and 24. The *Gentleman* makes a large Repetition of what he had ſaid before, wherein I obſerve nothing new, but that he ſaith, the *Eaſt-India Company* have Money at 4 *per cent*, only becauſe Men may have their Money out when they pleaſe, which is a miſtake, tho' a ſmall one; for the Company ſeldom or never take up Money but for a certain time, though I doubt not but that Generous *Company* will, and do at moſt times accommodate any Perſon with his Money before due, that hath occaſion to require ſuch a kindneſs of them, although they oblige not themſelves to do it.

In his Tenth Particular, at the latter end of Page 24. he ſaith, I am miſtaken in my Aſſertion of the Intereſt of *Scotland*, which upon further enquiry amongſt the *Scotch-Merchants* upon the *Exchange*, I am told is his own miſtake; ſo I muſt leave that being matter of Fact to thoſe that know that Country and its Laws, more and better than either of us: Laſtly, He concludes, that whilſt I ſay the matter in *England* is ſo naturally prepared for an Abatement of Intereſt, that it cannot be long obſtructed; I propound a Law to anticipate Nature, which is againſt Reaſon.

I

I anſwer, It was the wiſdom of our *Grand-Fathers* to bring it to what it would bear in their time; and our *Fathers* found the good effects of that, and brought it lower, and the benefit thereof is ſince manifeſted to us by the ſucceſs; and therefore ſeeing the matter will now bear further Abatement, it is reaſonable for us to follow that excellent Example of our *Anceſtors*; *Laws againſt Nature I grant would be ineffectual; but I never heard before, that Laws to help Nature were againſt Reaſon.*

Touching the *Gentleman's* Perſonal Reflections upon me, I ſhall ſay little; it appears ſufficiently by what I have writ, and his anſwer, that *I am an Advocate for Induſtry, he for Idleneſs:* It appears likewiſe to thoſe that know me in *London*, which are many, that I am ſo far from deſigning to engroſs Trade, that I am haſtening to convert what I can of my ſmall Eſtate that is Perſonal into real, ſuppoſing it to be my Intereſt ſo to do, before the Uſe of Money falls, which I conclude cannot long ſuſpend, and that then Land and Houſes muſt riſe; and I doubt it will appear, when this *Gentleman* is as well known as I am, that he is more an *Uſurer*, than an Owner of Land or manager of Trade at preſent; my ends have only been to ſerve my *Country*, which I can with a

ſincere

ſincere Heart declare, in the Preſence of *God* and *Men*: And that nothing elſe could have engaged me into this unpleaſing Controverſie, wherein I have given unwilling Offences to all my neareſt Relations, and knew at firſt that I muſt needs do ſo, moſt of them being ſuch as Age and Wiſdom hath Inſtructed rather to be *Box-keepers* than *Gameſters*.

I have before-mentioned the Judgment of the *French King* and *Court*, but intended not to recite the *Edict*, being it is at large in Sir *Thomas Culpepper* Senior, his laſt Treatiſe: yet, on ſecond Thoughts, conſidering all Men perhaps may not come to a ſight of that, and finding the ſaid *Edict* ſo comprehenſive of the whole matter of this Controverſie, I have here recited it:

The King by theſe Edicts had nothing relieved the neceſſities of the Nobility, if he had not provided for Uſuries, which have ruined many good and ancients Houſes; filled Towns with unprofitable Servants, and the Countries with Miſeries and Inhumanities; he found the Rents, viz. *Uſuries conſtituted after* 10 *or* 8 *in the Hundred, did Ruin many good Families, hindred the Traffick and Commerce of Merchandizes, and made Tillage and Handicrafts to be neglected, many deſiring through the eaſineſs of a deceitful Gain to live Idlely in good Towns of their*

their Rents, rather than give themselves with any Pains to Liberal Arts, or to Till or Husband their Inheritances: For this reason, meaning to invite his Subjects to Enrich themselves with more just Gain, to content themselves with more moderate Profit, and to give the Nobility means to pay their Debts, he did forbid all Usury to Constitution of Rent at an higher rate than six Pounds five Shillings in the Hundred.

The *Edict* was verified in the Court of *Parliament, which considered that it was always Prejudicial to the* Common-Wealth, *to give Money to Usury*; for it is a Serpent whose biting is not apparent, and yet it is so sensible, that it pierceth the very Hearts of the best Families.

The whole of this Controversie lies narrowly in these two short Questions, *viz. Will Abatement of Interest improve Trade?* Secondly, *Will it advance the Price of Land? The collective united Bodies of the Government of our own and other Kingdoms, expresly say it will do both; and Experience cries aloud that so it will do, and hath done, in all Ages and in all Places:* And I never yet met with any private Person, how much soever concerned in Interest, that had the ignorance or confidence to deny both.

For Discourse with a *Country Usurer*, he will affirm, and perhaps be ready to Swear

to

to it, that this Abatement of
Knavish Design of the Citizens
themselves, who are too Proud a
that if it go forward it will
Country *Gentlemen* in *England*:
speak with the *City Usurers*, th
ready to affirm, that this is a
on only by *Noblemen* and *Gentl*
Estates are all in Land, for th
vantage, and that it will spoil a
of the *Kingdom*, being a Project
stant to take off just one third
Estates that are Personal, and a
Proportion to all such whose
real; which in effect is to impo
Younger, and enrich all *Elder*
England: So that out of the M
greatest and wisest Adversaries
ciple, it may be justly conclud
singly they deny the truth of it,
they confess it.

To conclude, there is nothin
said, or that I think any other
this occasion, but was said in
fore by old Sir *Thomas Culpepper*
known to me) who had an amp
sight into the whole nature of th
and the true effects and conseq
Truth being always the same, thoug
may vary; nor can any thing

jected against the making a Law for a further Abatement of Interest, but the same that was objected in those times wherein the former *Statutes* past; so *that* why my *Opposer* should Cavil at the doing of that by a Law in *England* now (which he seems to like well, if it could be done) I know no real Cause, except it be that in truth he is wise enough to know that a Law in *England* will certainly do the work, as it hath done formerly, and in consequence his own private Gain will be Retrenched.

Before I conclude, I think it necessary, for Caution to my *Country-Men*, to let them know what effects these discourses have had on others; when I wrote my first Treatise, Interest was in the *Island* of *Barbadoes* at 15 *per cent*, where it is since by an Act of the *Country* brought down to 10 *per cent* (a great fall at once) and our weekly *Gazettes* did some Months past inform us, that the *Swedes* by a Law had brought down their Interest to 6 *per cent*; neither of which can have any good effects upon us, but certainly the contrary, except by way of Emulation they quicken us to provide in time for our own Good and Prosperity.

I have now done with this Controversie, and therein discharged my Duty to my native Country; and though Ignorance, Malice,

lice, or private Intereſt may yet for ſome time oppoſe it, *I am confident the Wiſdom of my Country-men will at length find their true and general Intereſt, in the Eſtabliſhment of ſuch a Law*, which, as to my own particular Concernments, ſignifies not two Farthings whether they do or not.

CHAP. II.

Concerning the Relief and Employment of the Poor.

THis is a calm Subject, and thwarts no common or private Intereſt amongſt us, except that of the common Enemy of Mankind (the *Devil*) ſo I hope that what ſhall be offered towards the effecting of ſo univerſally acceptable a Work as this, and the removal of the innumerable Inconveniences that do now and have in all Ages attended this Kingdom, through defect of ſuch Proviſion for the Poor, will not be ill taken, although the Plaiſter at firſt Eſſay do not exactly fit the Sore.

In

In the Discourse of this subject, I shall first assert some particulars, which I think are agreed by common Consent, and from thence take occasion to proceed to what is more doubtful.

1. *That our Poor in* England *have always been in a most sad and wretched condition*; some Famished for want of Bread, others Starved with Cold and Nakedness, and many whole Families in all the out Parts of Cities and great Towns, commonly remain in a languishing nasty and useless Condition, Uncomfortable to themselves, and Unprofitable to the Kingdom; this is confessed and lamented by all Men.

2. That the *Children* of our *Poor* bred up in *Beggery* and *Laziness*, do by that means become not only of *unhealthy Bodies*, and more than ordinarily subject to many loathsome Diseases, whereof very many die in their tender Age; and if any of them do arrive to years and strength, they are, by their Idle habits contracted in their Youth, rendered for ever after indisposed to Labour, and serve only to stock the *Kingdom* with *Thieves* and *Beggars*.

3. *That if all our impotent Poor were provided for, and those of both Sexes and all Ages that can do work of any kind employed, it would redound some Hundreds of Thousands of Pounds*

per Annum *to the Publick Advantage.*

4. *That it is our Duty to God and Nature, so to Provide for, and employ the Poor.*

5. *That by so doing one of the great sins (for which this land ought to mourn) would be removed.*

6. *That our fore-Fathers had pious Intentions towards this good Work, as appears by the many Statutes made by them to this purpose.*

7. *That there are places in the World where-in the Poor are so provided for, and employed, as in* Holland, Hambrough, New-England *and others, and, as I am informed, now in the* City *of* Paris.

Thus far we all agree: The first Question then that naturally occurs is,

Question, *How comes it to pass that in* England *we do not nor ever did comfortably maintain and employ our Poor?*

The common Answers to this Question are, two.

1. *That our Laws to this purpose are as good as any in the World, but we fail in the execution.*

2. *That formerly in the days of our pious Ancestors the work was done, but now Charity is decreased;* and that is the reason we see the Poor so neglected as now they are.

In both which Answers (I humbly conceive) the effect is mistaken for the Cause: For though it cannot be denied, but there hath been, and is a great failure in the Execution

cution of thoſe *Statutes* which relate to the *Poor*, yet I ſay, the *cauſe of that failure hath been occaſioned by defect of the Laws themſelves.*

For otherwiſe, what is the reaſon that in our late times of Confuſion and Alteration, wherein almoſt every party in the Nation, at one time or other, took their turn at the Helm, and all had that Compaſs (thoſe Laws) to Steer by, and yet none of them could, or ever did, conduct the Poor into a Harbour of ſecurity to them, and profit to the Kingdom, i. e. *none ſufficiently maintained the Impotent, and employed the Indigent amongſt us:* And if this was never done in any Age, nor by any ſort of Men whatſoever, in this Kingdom, who had the uſe of thoſe Laws now in force, it ſeems to me a very ſtrong Argument that it never could, nor ever will be done by thoſe Laws, and that conſequently the defect lies in the Laws themſelves, not in the Men, *i. e.* thoſe that ſhould put them in Execution.

As to the ſecond Anſwer to the aforeſaid Queſtion, wherein *want of Charity* is aſſigned for another cauſe why the *Poor* are now ſo much neglected, I think it is a *Scandalous, ungrounded Accuſation* of our *Contemporaries* (except in relation to building of *Churches*, which I confeſs this generation is not ſo

Propenſe to, as former have been) for moſt that I converſe with, are not ſo much troubled to part with their Money, as how to place it, that it may do good, and not hurt to the Kingdom: For, *If they give to the Beggars in the Streets, or at their Doors, they fear they may do hurt by* encouraging that lazy unprofitable kind of Life; and *if they give more than their proportions in their reſpective Pariſhes, that* (they ſay) *is but giving to the Rich*, for the Poor are not ſet on Work thereby, nor have the more given them; but only their rich Neighbours pay the leſs. And for what was given in *Churches* to the *viſited Poor*, and to ſuch as were *impoveriſhed by the Fire*; we have heard of ſo many and great Abuſes of that kind of *Charity*, that moſt Men are under ſad diſcouragements in relation thereunto.

I Write not this to divert any Man from Works of Charity of any kind: *He that gives to any in want does well; but he that gives to Employ and Educate the Poor, ſo as to render them uſeful to the Kingdom, in my judgment does better.*

And here by the way, not to leave Men at a loſs how to diſpoſe of what God ſhall incline their Hearts to give for the benefit of the Poor, I think it not impertinent to propoſe the *Hoſpitals* of this City, and *Poor labour-*

bouring People that have many Children, and make a hard ſhift to ſuſtain them by their induſtry, whereof there are multitudes in the out Parts of this *City*; *as the beſt objects of Charity at preſent.*

But to return to my purpoſe, *viz.* to prove that the want of *Charity* likewiſe that is now, and always hath been, in relation *to the Poor*, *proceeds from a defect in our Laws.* Ask any Charitable minded Man as he goes along the Streets of *London*, viewing the Poor, viz. *Boys*, *Girls*, *Men and Women* of all Ages, and many in good Health, &c. why he and others do not take care for the ſetting thoſe Poor Creatures to Work? Will he not readily anſwer, that he wiſheth heartily it could be done, tho' it coſt him a great part of his Eſtate, but he is but one Man, and can do nothing towards it; *giving them Money*, *as hath been ſaid*, *being but to bring them into a liking and continuance in that way.*

The ſecond Queſtion then is,

Queſtion 2. *Wherein lies the defect of our preſent Laws relating to the Poor?*

I anſwer, that there may be many, but I ſhall here take notice of one only, which I think to be Fundamental, and which untill altered, the *Poor* in *England* can never be well provided for, or Employed; and that when the ſaid Fundamental Error is well amended, it is almost impossible they should lack either Work or Maintenance.

The said radical Error I esteem to be the leaving it to the care of every Parish to maintain their own Poor only; upon which follows the shifting off, sending or whiping back the Poor Wanderers to the place of their Birth, or last abode: The practice whereof I have seen many years in *London*, to signifie as much as ever it will, which is just nothing of good to the Kingdom in general, or the Poor thereof, tho' it be sometimes by accident to some of them a Punishment without effect; I say without effect, because it reforms not the Party, nor disposeth the minds of others to Obedience, which are the true ends of all Punishment.

As for instance, *a Poor idle Person*, that will not Work, or that no Body will Employ in the Country, *comes up to* London *to set up the Trade of Begging*; such a person probably may Beg up and down the Streets seven years, it may be seven and twenty, before any body asketh why she doth so, and if at length she hath the ill hap in some Parish, to meet with a more vigilant *Beadle* than one of twenty of them are, all he does is but to lead her the length of five or six Houses into another Parish, and then concludes, as his *Masters* the *Parishioners* do, that he hath done

done the part of a most diligent Officer: but suppose he should yet go further to the end of his Line, which is the end of the Law; and the perfect Execution of his Office; that is, suppose he should carry this poor wretch to a Justice of the Peace, and he should order the *Delinquent* to be Whipt, and sent from Parish to Parish, to the place of her *Birth* or last *Abode*, which not one *Justice* of twenty (through pity or other cause) will do; even this is a great charge upon the Country, and yet the business of the Nation it self wholly undone: For no sooner doth the *Delinquent* arrive at the place assigned, but for shame or idleness she presently deserts it, and wanders directly back, or some other way, hoping for better fortune, whilst the Parish to which she is sent, knowing her a Lazy, and perhaps a worse qualify'd person, is as willing to be rid of her, as she is to be gone from thence.

If it be here retorted upon me, that by my own Confession, much of this mischief happens by the non, or ill Execution of the Laws; I say better Execution than you have seen you must not expect; and *there was never a good Law made that was not well executed, the fault of the Law causing a failure of execution*, it being natural to all Men to use the remedy next at hand, and rest satisfied with shifting the Evil from their own Doors; which in regard they can so easily do, by threatning or thrusting a Poor Body out of the verge of their own *Parish*, it is unreasonable and vain to hope that ever it will be otherwise.

For the Laws against Inmates, and empowering the Parishoners to take Security before they suffer any Poor Person to Inhabit amongst them; it may be they were prudent Constitution, at the times they were made (and before *England* was a place of Trade) and may be so still in some Countries, but *I am sure in Cities and great Towns of Trade they are altogether improper, and contrary to the practice of other Cities and Trading Towns abroad.* The Riches of a *City*, as of a *Nation*, consisting in the multitude of *Inhabitants*; and if so, you must allow *Inmates, or have a City of Cottages.* And if a right course be taken for the sustentation of the *Poor*, and setting them on Work, you need invent no Stratagems to keep them out, but rather to bring them in. For *the resort of Poor to a City or Nation well managed, is in effect the conflux of Riches to that City or Nation*; and therefore the subtile *Dutch* receive, and relieve, or employ all that come to them, not enquiring what Nation, much less what Parish they are of.

Question

Question 3. The third Question: *If the defect be in our Laws, how shall we find a remedy that may be rational and consistent?*

This I confess is a hard and difficult question, it is one of the *Ardua Regni*, and may very well deserve the most deliberate consideration of our wisest *Councellors*. And if a whole Session of *Parliament* were employed on this singular concern, I think it would be time spent as much to the Glory of *God* and good of this *Nation*, as in any thing that noble and worthy *Patriots* of their Country can be engaged in: But seeing I have adventured thus far, I shall humbly proceed to offer some general proposals that have a tendency towards the effecting this great Work, which being seriously thought of and debated by wiser Men, may be capable of such melioration as may render them in a great measure effectual to the *Kingdom* in general; altho' at present, to prevent that common Objection, that great Mutations are dangerous; I shall only propose them to be experimented in these parts of the Kingdom, which are the Vitals of our body politick, which being once made sound, the cure of the rest will not be difficult.

Proposition 1. First then I propose, *That the City of* London *and* Westminster, *Burrough of* Southwark, *and all other places with-*

in

in the usual Lines of Communication, described in the Weekly Bills of Mortality, *may by Act of Parliament be associated into one Province, or Line of Communication for relief of the Poor.*

2. *That there be one Assembly of Men* (and such as they shall from time to time appoint and deputise) *entrusted with the care for, and treasure of, all the poor within the said pale or Line of Communication.*

3. *That the said Assembly be incorporated by Act of Parliament*, with perpetual Succession, by the name of *Fathers of the Poor*, or some other honourable and significant Title.

4. *That all Constables, Church-wardens, Overseers, or other Officers in all Parishes*, within the said Line, *be subordinate and accountable to the said Fathers of the Poor, and their Deputies for, and in all things relating to, the Poor.*

5. *That the said Fathers of the Poor may have liberty to assess and receive into their common Treasury*, for relief of their Poor, *so much Money from every Parish, as they yearly paid to that purpose, any of the three Years preceeding this Constitution, and to compel the payment thereof, but not of more.*

6. *That the said Fathers of the Poor, and their Deputies may have very large and sufficient power in all things relating to the Poor*, and particularly to have and receive the charitable benevolence of all persons once every Lords Day in every

Church, and in any other Meet-
Christians, and at any other
which they ſhall think fit.

ſaid Fathers of the Poor, and
hall authoriſe, *may have power*
nds, erect and endow Work-houſes,
Houſes of Correction, and to ex-
r Powers relating to the Poor,
ber of *Juſtices* of the *Peace* now
heir *Quarter-Seſſions*, or other-

ſaid Fathers of the Poor may have
ſuch Poor beyond the Seas as they
nto his Majeſties Plantations, ta-
for their confortable Mainte-
their ſervice, and for their
wards.

ſaid Fathers of the Poor may have
etty Banks and Lumbards for the
or, if they ſhall find it convenient,
eceive the one half of what is
he Doors of *Play-houſes*, and
t for *Farthings*, and to do what-
Majeſty and *Parliament* ſhall
ecommend to them, or leave
etion.

Treaſure that ſhall be Collected
e ſhall be accounted ſacred, and
ony to miſapply, conceal, lend
to any other uſe or purpoſe

II.

11. *That there be no Oaths, or other Tests imposed upon the said Fathers of the Poor, at their admission, to barr our Nonconformists*, amongst whom there will be found some excellent Instruments for this good Work, and such as will constantly attend it (for if they be kept out, the People will be cold in their Charity, and in their hopes of the success.)

12. *That the said Fathers of the Poor may constantly wear some honourable Meddal*, such as the *King* and *Parliament shall devise*, besides the *green Staff* which is now used in *London* to such like purpose (but upon extraordinary days only) *to denote their Authority and Office*, at all times, and in all places, after the manner of the Habits in *Spain*, or rather as have all the *Familiars* of the *Inquisition* in most *Romish* Countries, with admirable effect, though to a wicked purpose; the consequence whereof will be, that the said *Fathers of the Poor*, being numerous, and disperst by their Habitations and Business, into most parts of their *Province*, will readily see any neglects of Officers, and as easily redress them; the *Meddal* which they wear about them, being a sufficient Warrant to command Obedience from all *Parish-Officers* where-ever they come, altho' their Persons be not known there.

13. *That the said Fathers of the Poor may have*

have liberty to admit into their Society and all Powers and Priviledges equal with them, any persons that are willing to serve God, their King and Country, in this pious and publick Work, the persons desiring to be so admitted, paying at their admission 100 *l.* or more into the Poors Treasury, as a demonstration of the sincerity of their Intentions to labour in and cultivate this most Religious Vineyard. This I only offer because the number of the said *Fathers of the Poor* hereafter mentioned, may be thought rather too few than too many.

14. *That the said Fathers of the Poor, besides the Authority now exercised by Justices of the Peace, may have some less limited Powers given them, in relation to the punishment of their own and Parish-Officers, by pecuniary mulcts for the Poors benefit in case of neglect*, and otherwise as his *Majesty* and the *Parliament* shall think fit.

15. *That the said Fathers of the Poor may have freedom to set the Poor on work about whatsoever Manufacture they think fit*, with a *Non-obstante* to all Patents that have been or shall be granted to any private Person or Persons for the sole Manufacture of any Commodity; the want of which Priviledge, I have been told, was a prejudice to the Work-house at *Clerkenwell*, in their late design of setting their Poor Children about making of *Hangings*.

16.

16. *That all Vacancies by reason of death of any of the said Fathers of the Poor be perpetually supplied by election of the Survivors.*

Quest. 4. The fourth Question is, *who shall be the Persons entrusted with so great a Work, and such excess of Power.*

This is a Question likewise of some difficulty, and the more in regard of our present Differences in *Religion*; but I shall answer it as well as I can.

In general I say, *They must be such as the People must have ample satisfaction in, or else the whole design will be lost:* For if the universality of the People be not satisfied with the Persons, they will never part with their Money; but if they be well satisfied therein they will be miraculously Charitable.

Quest. 5. This begets a fifth Question *viz. What sort of Men the People will be most satisfied in?*

I answer, I think *in none so well as such only as a common Hall of the Livery-men of* London *shall make choice of*; it being evident by the experience of many Ages, that the several *Corporations* in *London* are the best *Administrators* of what is left to *charitable Uses*, that have ever been in this *Kingdom*, which is manifest in the regular, Just and Prudent management of the *Hospitals* of *London*, and was wisely observed by *Doctor Collet, Dean*

of

of St. Paul's, that prudent *Ecclesiastick*, when he left the Government of that *School*, and other great Revenues assigned by him for charitable Uses, unto the disposition of the *Mercers Company*.

Object. But here it may be objected, That *Country-Gentlemen*, who have Power in places of their Residences, and pay out of their large Estates considerable sums towards the Maintenance of their Poor within the aforelimited Precincts, may be justly offended if they likewise have not a share in the distribution of what shall be raised to that purpose.

Answ. I answer, the force of this objection may be much taken off, if the *City* be obliged to choose but a certain number out of the *City*, as suppose seventy for *London*, ten out of *Southwark* for that Burrough, twenty for *Westminster*, this would best satisfie the People, and I think do the Work: But if it be thought too much for the *City* to have the choice of any more than their own seventy, the *Justices* of *Peace* in their *Quarter-Sessions*, may nominate and appoint their own number of Persons to assist for their respective Jurisdictions, and so to supply the vacancy in case of Death, *&c.* But all must be conjunctive, but one *Body politick*, or the work will never be done.

Quest.

Quest. 6. The sixth Question is, *What will be the advantage to the Kingdom in general, and to the Poor in particular, that will accrue by such a Society of Men, more than is enjoyned by the Laws at present?*

I answer, innumerable and unspeakable are the Benefits of this Kingdom that will arise from the Consultations and debates of such a wise and honest Council, who being Men so elected as aforesaid, will certainly conscionably study and labour to discharge their trust in this service of *God*, their *King* and *Country*.

1. *The Poor, of what quality soever, as soon as they are met with, will be immediatly relieved or set on work where they are found, without hurrying them from place to place, and torturing their Bodies to no purpose.*

2. *Charitable-minded-men will know certainly where to dispose of their Charity, so as it may be employed to right purposes.*

3. *House-keepers will be freed from the intollerable incumbrance of Beggars at their Doors.*

4. *The Plantations will be regularly supplied with Servants, and those that are sent thither well provided for.*

5. *The said Assembly will doubtless appoint some of their own Members to visit and relieve such as are sick*, as often as there shall be occasion, together with Poor Labouring Families both in *City* and *Suburbs*.

6. *Poor*

6. *Poor Children will be Instructed in Learning and Arts*, and thereby rendered serviceable to their Country, and many other worthy Acts done for publick Good by the joynt Deliberation of so many prudent and pious Men, assisted with such a Power and Purse, more than can be fore-seen or expressed by a private Person.

Quest. 7. The Seventh Question may be, *What shall all the Poor of these Cities and Countries, being very numerous, be employed about?*

This Question will be answer'd best by the said Assembly themselves, when they have met and consulted together, who cannot be presumed deficient of Invention to set all the Poor on Work, especially since they may easily have admirable Presidents from the Practice of *Holland* in this particular, and have already very good ones of their own, in the Orders of their *Hospitals* of *Christ's-Church* and *Bridewell* in *London*; the *Girls may be employed in mending the Cloaths of the Aged, in Spinning, Carding, and other Linnen Manufactures, and many in Sowing Linnen for the* Exchange, *or any House-keepers that will put out Linnen to the Matrons that have the Government of them.*

The Boys in picking Okam, making Pins, Rasping Wood, making Hangings, or any other Manufactures of any kind; which whether it turns to present Profit or not, is not much material, the great Business of the Nation being first but to keep the Poor from Begging and Starving, and inuring such as are able to Labour and Discipline, that they may be hereafter useful Members to the Kingdom: But to conclude, I say the Wisest Man, living Solitarily, cannot propose or imagine such excellent Ways and Methods as will be Invented by the united Wisdom of so Grave an *Assembly*.

The sitting of the said *Assembly*, I humbly conceive, ought to be, *De die in diem*; the *Quorum* not more than Thirteen; whether they shall Yearly, Monthly or Weekly choose a *President*, how they shall distribute themselves into the several quarters of the *Communication*, what *Treasurers* and other *Officers* to employ, and where, and how many, will best be determined by themselves, and that without difficulty, because many that will probably be Members of the said *Assembly*, have already had large Experience of the Government of the *Hospitals* of *London*: The manner of Election of the said *Fathers of the Poor*, I humbly suppose cannot possibly be better contrived than after the same way which the *East-India Company* choose their *Committee*, which will prevent the Confusion, Irregularity and Incertitude

certitude that may attend the Election of Voices, or holding up of Hands; especially because the Persons to be elected at one time will be very many. The said manner proposed is, every *Elector, viz.* every *Livery Man* to bring to *Guild-hall* at the appointed day for Elections, a List of the whole number of Persons, such as he thinks fit, that are to be Elected, and deliver the same openly unto such Persons as the *Lord Mayor, Aldermen* and *Common-Council Men* shall appoint to make the Scrutiny; which Persons so entrusted, with the said Scrutiny, seven or ten days after, as shall be thought fit, at another *Common-hall* may declare who are the Persons Elected by the Majority of Votes.

If it be here objected to the whole purpose of this Treatise, that this work may as well be done in distinct *Parishes*, if all *Parishes* were obliged to build *Work-houses*, and employ their Poor therein; as *Dorchester* and some others have done with good success.

I answer, That such attempts have been made in many Places to my knowledge, with very good intents and strenuous endeavours, but all, that ever I heard of, proved vain and ineffectual, as I fear will that of *Clerken-well*, except that single instance of the Town of *Dorchester*, which yet signifies nothing in relation to the Kingdom in general, becauſe all other places cannot do the like, nor doth the Town of *Dorcheſter* entertain any but their own Poor only, and Whip away all others; whereas that which I deſign is to propoſe ſuch a Foundation as ſhall be large, wiſe, honeſt and rich enough to maintain and employ all *Poor* that come within the Pale of their Communication, without enquiring where they were Born, or laſt Inhabited: Which I dare affirm with Humility, that nothing but a *National*, or at leaſt ſuch a *Provincial* Purſe can ſo well do, nor any Perſons in this Kingdom, but ſuch only as ſhall be pickt out by popular Election for the reaſon before alledged, *viz.* That, in my opinion, *three fourths* at leaſt of the *Stock* muſt iſſue from the Charity of the People; as I doubt not but it will to a greater Proportion, if they be ſatisfied in the *Managers* thereof; but if otherwiſe, not the fourtieth, I might ſay, not the hundredth part.

I propoſe the Majority of the ſaid *Fathers of the Poor* to be *Citizens* (*though I am none my ſelf*) becauſe I think a great ſhare of the Money to be employed, muſt and will come from them, if ever the Work be well done; as alſo, becauſe their Habitations are neareſt the Center of their Buſineſs, and they beſt acquainted with all Affairs of this nature,

by

by their Experience in the Government of the *Hospitals*.

Earnestly to desire and endeavour, that the Poor of *England* should be better provided for and employed, is a work that was much studied by my Deceased *Father*; and therefore though I be as ready to confess, as any shall be to charge me with, Disability to propose a Model of Laws for this great Affair, yet I hope the more Ingenious will pardon me for endeavouring to give aim towards it, since it is so much my duty, which in this particular I shall be careful to perform (though I may be too remiss in others) as shall appear by more visible and apparent demonstrations, if ever this design, or any other (that is like to effect what is desired) succeed.

Now I have adventured thus far, I shall proceed to publish my Thoughts and Observations concerning some other things that have Relation to Trade, which I do without any purpose or design, save only to give occasion to my *Country-men*, to be Discoursing and Meditating upon those things which have a tendency to publick Good, from whence (tho' my Suggestions should be mistakes) probably some good effect may ensue, and therefore the Ingenicus, I know, though they may differ from me, will not blame me for the attempt.

CHAP. III.

Concerning Companies of Merchants.

COmpanies of *Merchants* are of two sorts, *viz.* *Companies in joynt Stock*, such as the *East-India-Company*, the *Morea-Company* (which is a Branch of the *Turkey-Company*) and the *Greenland-Company*, which is a Branch of the *Muscovian-Company*; the other sort are *Companies* who Trade not by a *joynt Stock*, but only are under a Government and Regulation, such are the *Hambrough-Company*, the *Turkey-Company*, the *Eastland-Company*, the *Muscovia-Company*.

It hath for many Years been a Moote Case, whether any Encorporating of *Merchants*, be for publick Good or not.

For my own part, I am of Opinion,

That for *Countries* with which his *Majesty* hath no *Alliance*, nor can have any by reason

reason of their distance, or Barbarity, or Non-Communication with the *Princes* of *Christendom*, &c. where there is a necessity of Maintaining Forces and Forts (such as *East-India* and *Guinia*) *Companies* of *Merchants* are absolute necessary.

2. *It seems evident to me, that the greatest part of these two Trades ought for publick Good to be managed by joynt Stock.*

3. *It's questionable to me, whether any other Company of Merchants are for publick Good or Hurt.*

4. I conclude however, *that all Restrictions of Trade are naught*, and consequently that no *Company* whatsoever, whether they Trade in a *joynt Stock* or under *Regulation*, can be for Publick Good, except it may be easie for all, or any of his *Majesty's Subjects* to be admitted into all, or any of the said *Companies*, at any time, for a very inconsiderable Fine, and that if the Fine exceed 20 *l.* including all Charges of Admission, it is too much, and that for these Reasons :

1. Because the *Dutch* who thrive best by Trade, and have the surest Rules to thrive by, *admit not only any of their own* People, *but even* Jews *and all kind of* Aliens, *to be free of any of their Societies of* Merchants, *or any of their Cities or Towns Corporate.*

2. *Nothing in the World can enable us to*

coap with the Dutch *in any Trade, but encrease of Hands and Stock, which a general admission will do*; many Hands and much Stock being as necessary to the Prosperity of any Trade, as Men and Money to Warfare.

3. There is no pretence of any good to the Nation by *Companies*, but only *Order and Regulation* of Trade; and if that be preserved (which the admission of all that will come in and submit to the *Regulation*, will not Prejudice) all the good to the Nation that can be hoped for, by *Companies*, is obtained.

4. The *Eastland*, beside our *Native Commodities*, spend great quantities of *Italian, Spanish, Portugal* and *French Commodities*, viz. *Oyl, Wine, Fruit, Sugar, Succads, Shoomack*, &c. Now in regard our *East Country Merchants* of *England* are few, compared with the *Dutch*, and intend principally that one Trade out and home, and consequently are not so conversant in the aforesaid *Commodities*, nor forward to adventure upon them, and seeing that by the *Companies Charter* our *Italian, Spanish, Portugal* and *French Merchants*, who understand those *Commodities* perfectly well, are excluded those Trades, or at least, if the *Company* will give them leave to send out those Goods, are not permitted to bring in the Returns; it follows

lows, that the *Dutch* must supply *Denmark*, *Sweden*, and all parts of the *Baltique*, with most of those *Commodities*; and so it is in Fact.

5. The *Dutch* who have no *Eastland-Company*, yet have ten times the Trade to the *Eastern Parts* as we have; and for *Italy*, *Spain* and *Portugal*, where we have no *Companies*, we have yet left full as much, if not more, Trade, than the *Dutch*. And for *Russia* and *Greenland*, where we have *Companies* (and I think Establish'd by *Act* or *Acts* of *Parliament*) our Trade is in effect wholly lost, while the *Dutch* have, without *Companies*, encreased theirs to above Fourty times the Bulk of what the residue of ours now is.

From whence may be inferred,

1. *That restrained limited Companies are not alone sufficient to preserve and encrease a Trade.*

2. *That limited Companies, tho' Established by Act of Parliament, may lose a Trade.*

3. *That Trade may be carried on to any part of* Christendom, *and encreased, without* Companies.

4. *That we have declined more, at least have encreased less, in those Trades limited to* Companies, *than in others where all his Majesties Subjects have had equal freedom to Trade.*

The common *Objections* against this easie Admission of all his *Majesties Subjects* into *Companies* of *Merchants*, are:

Object.

Object. 1. If all Persons may come into any *Company* of *Merchants* on such easie terms, than Young *Gentlemen*, *Shop-keepers* and divers others will turn *Merchants*, who through their own unskilfulness will pay dear for our Native *Commodities* here, and sell them cheap abroad; and also buy Foreign *Commodities* dear abroad, and sell them here for less than their cost, to the Ruine of themselves, and Destruction of *Trade*.

I answer, First, **Caveat emptor**, Let particular Men look to themselves, and so doubtless they will in those Trades for which there are now *Companies*, as well as they do in others for which there are no *Companies*.

It is the care of *Law-Makers* first and principally, to provide for the People in gross, not particulars; and if the Consequence of so easie an Admission, should be to make our *Manufactures* cheap abroad, and *Foreign Commodities* cheap here (as is alledged) our *Nation* in general would have the advantage both ways.

Object. 2. *If all should be admitted*, &c. *Shop-keepers being the Retailers, of the same* Commodities *the* Company *Imports, would have so much the advantage of the Merchant, that they would beat the Merchant not wholly out of the Trade.*

I anſwer, Firſt, *We ſee no ſuch thing in* Holland, *nor in the open Trades*, viz. *France, Spain, Portugal, Italy*, and all our own *Plantations*, neither can that well be, for to drive a *Retail Trade* to any purpoſe, requires a Mans full Stock, as well as his full Attendance, and ſo doth it to drive the Trade of a *Merchant*, and therefore few can find Stock and time to attend both; from whence it follows, that of the many Hundreds which in memory have turned *Merchants*, very few continued long to follow both, but commonly, after two or three Years Experience, betake themſelves wholly to *Merchandizing*, or returned to the ſole Exerciſe of their *Retail way*; but whether they do, or do not, concerns not the Nation in general, whoſe common Intereſt is to buy cheap, whatever appellation the *Seller* hath, whether that of a meer *Merchant*, *Gentleman*. or a *Shop-keeper*.

Object. 3. If *Shop-keepers* and other Unexperienced Perſons may turn *Merchants*, &c. they will through Ignorance neglect buying and ſending out our *Native Manufactures*, and will ſend out our Money, or *Bills of Exchange*, to buy *Foreign Commodities*, which is an apparent National loſs.

I anſwer, That *Shop-keepers* are like all other Men (led by their profit) and if it be for their Advantage to ſend out *Manufactures*,

the

they will do it without forcing; and if it be for their Profit to send over Money or Bills of Exchange, they will do that, and so will *Merchants* as soon, and as much, as they.

Object. 4. *If any may be admitted*, &c. *what do we get by our Seven Years Service, and the great Sums of Money our Parents gave to Bind us Apprentices to* Merchants, *&c. And who will hereafter Bind his Son to a* Merchant?

I answer, *The end of Service and giving of Money with Apprentices, I have always understood to be the learning of the Art or Science of Merchandizing, not the Purchasing of an Immunity or Monopoly, to the Prejudice of our Country*; and that it is so, is evident from the Practice, there being many general *Merchants* that are free of no particular *Company*, who can have as large Sums of Money with Apprentices, as any other that are free of one or more particular *Companies of Merchants*; and many Merchants that are free of particular Companies, unto whom few will give any considerable Sums of Money with *Apprentices*; the Proportion of Money given with *Apprentices* not following the *Company* a *Merchant* is free of, but the condition of the Master, as to his more or less reputed Skill in his Calling, Thriving or going backward, greater or lesser Trade,

well

well or ill Government of himſelf and Family, &c.

Object. 5. *If all ſhould be admitted on ſuch eaſie terms, will not that be manifeſt injuſtice to the* Companies of Merchants, *who by themſelves or Predeceſſors have been at great Diſburſments to Purchaſe Priviledges and Immunities Abroad, as the* Turkey-Company, *and the* Hambrough-Company *have done.*

I anſwer, That I am yet to learn that any Company of Merchants not Trading with a Joyn Stock, ſuch as the *Turkey*, *Hambrough*, *Muſcovia* and *Eaſtland* Companies, ever Purchaſed their Priviledges, or Built and Maintained Forts, Caſtles, or Factories, or made any Wars at their own Charge; but I know the *Turkey* Company do maintain an Embaſſador and two Conſuls, and are ſometimes neceſſitated to make preſents to the *Grand Seignior*, or his great Officers; and the *Hambrough* Company are at ſome charge to maintain their Deputy, and Miniſter at *Hambrough*; and I think it would be great Injuſtice that any ſhould *Trade* to the places within their Charters, without paying the ſame Duties of Leviations towards the Companies charge as the preſent Adventurers do pay, but I know not why any ſhould be barred from Trading to thoſe places, or forced to pay a great Fine for Admiſſion, that

that are willing to pay the *Companies* Duties, and submit to the *Companies* Regulation and Orders in other respects.

Obj. 6. *If all may be admitted, as aforesaid, then such numbers of Shop-keepers and others would come into the Society of* Merchants, *as would by the Majority of Votes so much alter the Governours, Deputy and Assistants of the respective Companies, that Ignorant Persons would come into those ruling places, to the general prejudice of those Trades.*

I answer, *Those that make this Objection, if they be Merchants, know there is very little in it, for that it is not to be expected that twenty Shop-keepers will come into any one Company in a Year*; and therefore can have no considerable Influence upon the Elections; but if many more should come in, it would be the better for the *Nation*, and not the worse for the *Company*, for that all Men are led by their Interest; and it being the common Interest of all that engage in any Trade, that the Trade should be regulated and governed by wise, honest and able Men, there is no doubt but most Men will Vote for such as they esteem so to be, which is manifest in the *East-India Company*, where neither *Gentlemen nor Shop-keepers were at first excluded*, neither are they yet kept out; any *English-man whatsoever being permitted to come into*

that

that Company that will buy an Action, paying only five Pounds to the Company for his admission; and yet undeniable Experience hath convinced all Gain-sayers in this matter; that *Company*, since its having had so large and National a Foundation, having likewise had a succession of much better *Governours, Deputies* and *Assistants* than ever it had upon that narrow bottom it stood formerly, when none could be admitted to the freedom of that *Company*, for less than a Fine of *Fifty Pounds*; and the success hath been answerable, *For the first Company settled upon that narrow limited Interest, although their Stock was larger than this, decayed and finally came to Ruin and Destruction*; Whereas on the contrary, this being settled on more rational, and consequently more just, as well as more profitable Principles, *hath through God's Goodness thriven and encreased to the trebling of their first Stock.*

CHAP.

CHAP. IV.

Concerning the Act of *Navigation.*

THough this *Act* be by most concluded a very Beneficial Act for this *Kingdom*, especially by the *Masters* and *Owners* of *Shipping*, and by all *Sea-men*; yet some there are, both wise and honest *Gentlemen* and *Merchants*, that doubt whether the Inconveniences it hath brought with it, be not greater than the Conveniences.

For my own part, I am of opinion that in relation to *Trade*, *Shipping*, *Profit* and *Power*, it is one of the choicest and most prudent *Acts* that ever was made in *England*, and without which we had not now been *Owners* of one half the *Shipping*, nor *Trade*, nor *Employed*, one half the *Sea-men* which we do at present; but seeing time hath discovered some *Inconveniences* in it, if not *Defects*, which in my poor opinion do admit of an easie Amendment, and seeing that the whole *Act* is is not approved by unanimous Confent, I thought fit to Difcourfe a little concerning it, wherein after a plain method I fhall lay down fuch Objections as I have met with, and fubjoyn my Anfwers, with fuch Reafons as occur to my Memory in Confirmation of my own Opinion.

The *Objections* againft the whole *Act* are fuch as thefe;

Object. 1. Some have told me, That I on all occafions magnifie the *Dutch Policy* in relation to their Trade, and the *Dutch* have no *Act of Navigation*, and therefore they are certainly not always in the right, as to the understanding of their true Intereft in Trade, or elfe we are in the wrong in this.

I anfwer, I am yet to be informed where the *Dutch* have miffed their proper Intereft in Trade; but that which is fit for one Nation to do in relation to their Trade, is not fit for all; no more than the fame Policy is neceffary to a prevailing Army that are Mafters of the Field, as to an Army of lefs Force, to be able to encounter their Enemy at all times and places: The *Dutch by reafon of their great Stocks, low Intereft, multitude of Merchants and Shipping, are Mafters of the Field in Trade, and therefore have no need to build Caftles, Fortreffes and places of Retreat;* fuch I account Laws of Limitation, and Securing of Particular Trades to the *Natives* of any *Kingdom*; because they, *viz.* th *Dutch*, may be well assured, *That no Natio can enter in common with them in any Trade, gain Bread by it, while their own Use of Mon is at* 3 per cent, *and others at* 6 per cent *an upwards*, &c. Whereas if we should suff their Shipping in common with ours in tho Trades which are secured to the *English* E *Act of Navigation*, they must necessarily, i a few Years, for the reasons above-said, E us quite out of them.

Object. 2. The second *Objection* to th whole *Act* is; Some will confess that as *Merchants* and *Owners of Ships, the Act Navigation is eminently Beneficial*, but say, th *Merchants* and *Owners* are but an Inconsider ble number of Men in respect of the who *Nation*, and that Interest of the greater nu ber, that our *Native Commodities* and *Man factures* should be taken from us at the be Rates, and Foreign Commodities sold us the cheapest, with admission of *Dutch Me chants* and *Shipping in common with the* Engli by my own Implication would effect.

My answer is, That I cannot deny but th may be true, if the present Profit of t generality be barely and singly considere but this *Kingdom* being an *Island*, the defen whereof hath always been our *Shipping* a *Seamen*, it seems to me *absolutely necess*

ti

that Profit and Power ought joyntly to be consider'd, and if so, I think none can deny but the Act of *Navigation* hath and doth occasion building and employing three times the number of *Ships* and *Sea-men*, that otherwise we should or would do; and that consequently, *If our Force at Sea were so greatly impaired, it would expose us to the receiving of all kind of Injuries and Affronts from our Neighbours, and in conclusion render us a despicable and miserable People.*

Objections to several Parts of the Act of NAVIGATION.

Object. 1. *The Inhabitants and Planters of our Plantations in* America, *say, This Act will in time Ruin their Plantations, if they may not be permitted, at least, to carry their Sugars to the best Markets, and not be compelled to send all to, and receive all Commodities from* England.

I answer, *If they were not kept to the Rules of the Act of Navigation, the consequence would be, that in a few Years the Benefit of them would be wholly lost to the Nation*; It being agreeable to the Policy of the *Dutch*, *Danes*, *French*, *Spaniards*, *Portugals* and *all Nations in the World*, to keep their external *Provinces* and *Collonies* in a subjection unto, and de-

pendency upon their *Mother-Kingdom*; an
if they should not do so, the *Dutch*, who, as
have said, are Masters of the *Field* in Trade
would carry away the greatest of advantag
by the Plantations of all the Princes i
Christendom, leaving us and others only th
trouble of Breeding Men, and sending them
abroad to Cultivate the Ground, and hav
Bread for their Industry.

Here, by the way, with entire Submissio
to the greater Wisdom of those whom
much more concerns, give me leave to Qu
ry, *Whether, instead of the late Prohibition*
Irish *Cattle, it would not have been more f*
the Benefit of this Kingdom of England, *to suff*
the Irish *to bring into* England, *not only the*
Live Cattle, but also all other Commodities
the Growth or Manufacture of that Kingdo
Custom free, or on easie Customs, and to prohib
them from Trading home-ward or outward wi
the Dutch, *or our own Plantations, or any oth*
places, except the Kingdom of England? *M*
certainly such a Law would in a few Ye
wonderfully encrease the Trade, Shipping, a
Riches of this Nation.

Query 2. *Would not this be a good Additi*
to the Act of Navigation, and much encrease t
employment of English *Shipping and Sea-men,*
well in bringing from thence all the Commodit
of that Country, as supplying that Country w

Des

eals, Salt, *and all other Foreign Commodities* *hich now they have from the* Dutch?

Que. 3. *Would not this be a means effectually prevent the Exportation of* Irish *Wool, which w goes frequently into* France *and* Holland, *the manifest and great Damage both of* England *and* Ireland?

Que. 4. *Would not this be a Fortress or Law secure to us the whole Trade of* Ireland?

Que. 5. *Would not this render that which ow diminisheth, and seems Dangerous to, the alue of Lands in* England, *viz. The growth* Ireland, *advantagious, by encrease of Trade nd Shipping, and consequently the Power of this ingdom?*

Object. 2. The second *Objection* to part of 1e *Act of Navigation*, is usually made by 1e *Eastland* and *Norway Merchants*, who firm, that in effect their Trade is much eclined since the passing the *Act of Navigaon*; and the *Danes*, *Swedes*, *Holsteners*, and l *Easterlings*, who by the said *Act* may Import *Timber* and other *Eastern Commodities*, ave encreased in the number of their *Shipng*, imployed in this Trade, since our *Act* of *Navigation*, at least two third parts; and the *nglish* have proportionably declined in the umber of theirs imployed in that *Trade*.

I answer, That I believe the matter of act Asserted is true, as well as the cause

 assigned,

assigned, *viz.* the *Act of Navigation*; and yet this should not make us out of love with that excellent Law, rather let it put us upon contriving the Amendment of this seeming Defect, or Inconvenience, the Cure whereof, I hope upon mature Consideration, will not be found difficult, for which I humbly Propound to the *Wisdom of Parliament*, *viz.* That a *Law* be made to impose a *Custom* of at least 30 or 25 *l. per cent*, on all *Eastland Commodities*, *Timber*, *Boards*, *Pipe-staves and Salt Imported into* England *and* Ireland *upon any Ships but* English *Built Ships*; or at least such only as are Sailed with an *English Master* and at least three fourths *English Mariners*.

And that for these *Reasons*;

Reason First; *If this be not done, the* Danes Swedes *and* Easterlings *will certainly in a few Years carry the whole Trade*, by reason of the difference of the Charge of Building a *Ship* fit for that Trade there or here, *viz.* a *Fly-boat* of 300 Tuns new *Built*, and set to Sea for such a Voyage, may cost there 13 or 1400 which here would cost from 22 to 2400 which is so vast a Disproportion, that it impossible for an *English man* to coap with a *Dane* in that *Navigation* under such a Discouragement; to ballance which there nothing but the *Stranger's Duty* which the *Dane* now pays, which may come to 5 or 6 er Ship, *per* Voyage, at most, one with another, which is *Incompatible* with the difference of Price between the first cost of the Ships in either Nation. And this is so evident to those who are conversant in those Trades, that besides the decrease of our Shipping, and encrease of theirs that hath already happened, ours in Probability had been wholly beaten out of the Trade, and only *Danes* and *Easterlings* freighted, had we been necessitated to Build *English* Ships, and had not been recruited on moderate Prices by *Fly-boats* (being Ships proper for this Trade) taken in the late *Dutch War*, and by a further supply of *Scotch* Prizes likewise, through his *Majesties* Permission and Indulgence.

Reas. 2. Because the number of *Strangers* Ships Imployed in the aforesaid *Trade* Yearly, I estimate to be about two hundred Sail; which if such a Law were made, must unavoidably be all Excluded, and the Employment fall wholly into *English* Hands; which would be an Excellent Nursery, and give constant Maintenance to a brave Number of *English Sea-men*, more than we can or do employ at present.

Reas. 3. *The Act of Navigation is now of Seventeen or Eighteen Years standing in* England; *and yet in all these Years, very few, if any,*

English *Ships have been Built fit for this Trade*, the reason whereof is that before mentioned, *viz.* That it is cheaper freighting of *Danes* and *Easterlings*; and it being so, and all Men naturally led by their Profit, it seems to me in vain to expect that ever this *Law* will procure the Building of one *English* Ship fit for that employment, till those *Strangers* are excluded this *Trade* for *England*; and much more improbable it is, that any should now be Built, than it was formerly, when the *Act* was first made, because *Timber* is now at almost double the price in *England* it was then, *The consequence whereof is, That if timely Provision be not made by some additional Law, when our old Stock of* Flemish *Prizes is worn out, as many of them are already, we shall have very few or no Ships in this Trade.*

The *Objections* which I have heard made to this *Proposition* are, *viz.*

Object. 1. If such an *Imposition* be laid on those gross *Commodities* imported by *Strangers Ships*, that will amount to the excluding all *Strangers* from this Trade; we shall want Ships in *England* to carry on the Trade, and so the Commodity will not be had, or else will come very dear to us.

I answer, If the *Commodity* should be somewhat dearer for the present, it would be no loss to the *Nation* in general, because all *Freight*

Freight would be paid to *English Men*; whereas the *Freight* paid to *Serangers* (which upon those Commodities is commonly as much or more than the value of Goods) is all clear loss to the *Nation*.

2*dly*, If there should be a present want of Shipping, and the *Parliament* shall please to enjoyn us to Build *English* Ships for this Trade; This extraordinary good Effect will follow, *viz*.

It will engage us to do that we never yet did, *viz*. To fall to Building of *Fly-boats* (great Ships of burthen, of no force, and small charge in Sailing) which would be the most Profitable Undertaking that ever *English Men* were engaged in, and that which is absolutely necessary to be done, if ever we intend to board the *Dutch* in their *Trade* and *Navigation*; these *Fly-boats being the Milk-Cows of* Holland, *from which they have sucked manifoldly greater Profit than from all their Ships of force*; though both I know are necessary: But if at first the *Parljament* shall think fit to enjoyn us only to Ships Sailed with an *English Master*, and three fourths *English Mariners*, the *Danes* and *Easterlings* being by this means put out of so great an Employment for this Shipping, we shall buy Ships proper for this Trade on easie Terms of them, perhaps for half their cost, which under-

undervalue in Purchase will be a present clear Profit to *England*.

Object. 2. If this be done in *England*, may not other *Princes* account it hard and unreasonable, and consequently Retaliate the like upon us?

To answer this *Objection*, it's necessary to enquire what *Kingdom* and *Country* will be concerned in this *Law*.

1*st* Then, *Italy*, *Spain* and *Portugal* will be wholly Unconcerned:

2*dly*, So will *French*; who, if they were concerned, can take no offence, while they lay an *Imposition* of 50 or 60 *per cent* upon our *Drapery*.

3*dly*, The *Dutch* and *Hamburgers* would not by such additional Law be more excluded than now they are, and the latter would have an advantage by it, in case the *Danes* should (as it may be supposed they will) lay a *Tax* upon our Shipping there; for the consequence thereof would be, that much of those kind of Commodities we should fetch from *Hambrough*, where they are plentifully to be had, though at a little dearer Rate, and yet not so dear, but that the *Dutch* fetch Yearly thence 350 or 400 *Ships* Loading of *Timber*, and other *Wooden Commodities*.

4*thly*,

4*thly*, The *Swedes* would have an apparent Benefit by it, by turning a great part of the Stream of our Trade for those Commodities to *Gottenborow*, and divers other parts of *Sweden*, that are lately opened, and now opening, where very large quantities of *Timber*, *Masts* and *Boards* likewise may be had, though some small matter dearer than in *Norway*: Besides, if the *Swedes* should expect no advantage, but rather loss, by such amendment of our own *Laws*, they have no reason to be angry, because they have lately made so many *Laws* for Encouragement of their own *Shipping* and *Navigation*, and consequently Discouragement of ours, that do in effect amount to a Prohibition of the *English* from sending their own *Manufactures* to *Sweden* in *English Shipping*, insomuch that the *English Merchants*, when *Swedish* Shipping doth not present, are forced many times to send their Goods to *Elsinore*, to lye there till a *Swedish* Ship come by to put them aboard of, and pay their Factoridge, and other Charges; because if they should send them on *English Ships*, the Duties are so high in *Sweden*, that it is impossible for them to make their first cost of them.

5*thly*, The *Easterling* or *Hans-Towns*, tho' they were excluded this Trade for *England*

with

with their Shipping, whereof they have little (the greatest share being carried away by the *Danes*) would be gainers by the encrease of our Trade with them, for *Boards*, *Timber*, *Spruce Deals*, &c. at *Dantzick*, *Quinsborough*, and other places, which would be very considerable in case the *King* of *Denmark* should impose any considerable Extraordinary Tribute on our Shipping; which brings me to the third *Objection*.

Object. 3. If this be done, will not the *King* of *Denmark* lay a great *Imposition* upon all our *Shipping* that Trade into his *Dominions*, and also upon our *Drapery*, and other Native *English* Commodities.

I answer, That whatever that *King* may do at first, I am perswaded after he hath considered of it, he will be moderate in his *Impositions*, because he can hurt none but himself by making them great; for as to *Drapery*, and other *English* Goods, his Country spends none worth speaking of, and that charged with about 30 or 40 *per cent Custom* already; nine tenths of all the *Timber* and *Boards* we fetch from thence, being, in my opinion, Purchased with ready *Dollars* sent from *England* and *Holland*; and if he should by a great *Imposition* totally Discourage us from Trading with his People, we should lay out that Money with the *Swedes*, *Hamburgers*,

burgers, *Dantzickers*, and others, where we may have sufficient supply, while the *Danes* would be exceedingly Burthened with the lying of their Goods upon their Hands; there being in *Norway* great quantities of Goods, *viz.* The Course *Hemlock*, *Timber*, commonly brought from *Larwick*, *Tunsberry*, *Sandyford*, *Oskestrand*, *Hollumstrand*, and many other parts, which no *Nation* in the World Trades with them for, or will buy or use, but the *English* only.

CHAP. V.

Concerning Transferrence of Debts.

THE great Advantage that would accrue to this *Kingdom*, *by a Law for Transferring Bills of Debt*, from one Person to another, is sufficiently understood by most Men, especially by *Merchants*.

The difficulty seems not to be so much in making of a *Law* to this purpose, as reducing it it to practice, because we have been so long accustomed to buy and sell Goods by verbal Contracts only, that Rich and great Men for some time will be apt to think it a Diminution of their Reputation; to have Bills under their Hands and Seals demanded of them for Goods bought; and meaner Men will fear the loosing of their Customers, by insisting upon having such Bills for what they sell; which Inconveniency probably may be avoided, and the Good hoped for fully attained, if it be Enacted:

1. *That all and every Person and Persons, Native and Foreign, Bodies Politick and Corporate, Being or Inhabiting within the Kingdom of* England, *or Dominion of* Wales, *who from and after the day of* *shall buy and receive any Wares, Goods and Merchandize from any others, shall immediately on receipt thereof (in case ready money be not paid for the same) give unto him or them of whom such Goods, Wares and Merchandize shall be bought, or to his and their use, a Bill or Writing obligatory, under the Hand and Seal of him or them so buying the same, which shall mention the quality of the said Goods, and the neat sum of money, with the time or times of payment agreed upon.*

2. *That all Persons*, &c. *may Transfer the said Bills under their Hands to any other, by a short assignation on the back side.*

3. *That*

3. *That every such Assignee may Re-assign* **toties quoties.**

4. *After such Assignment, it shall not be in the power of any Assignor to make void, release or discharge the Debt.*

5. *No Debts after Assignment, to be liable to any Attachments, Execution, Statute or Commission of Bankrupt, or other Demand, as the Estate of him or them that Assigned the same.*

6. *That each Assignment shall absolutely vest the Property into the Assignee, to all intents and purposes.*

7. *That such Assignments being received, and Receipts or Discharges given for the same, shall be deemed good Payment.*

8. *That all Goods sold above the value of* 10 *l. after the day of for which no such Bill or Writing obligatory shall be given or tendred as aforesaid, to the Seller or Sellers thereof, or to his or their Use, shall be deemed and construed to all intents and purposes in the Law, as if the same had been Contracted for to be paid in ready Money, any Concession or Verbal Agreement between the said Parties to the contrary notwithstanding.*

This Clause I hope may be effectual to initiate us to a practice and observance of such a Law.

9. *That the first Assignment of any such Bill or Bills of Debt, be to this or the like effect.*

I A, B. Do engage and atteſt, that the *Debt*, within mentioned, is a true *Debt*, and no part of it paid to me, or to my uſe, or diſcharged by me; and I do hereby Aſſign over the ſame to *C. D.* for his own Account.

10. *And that the ſecond, and all other after Aſſignations upon any ſuch Bills, ſhall be to this or the like effect*, viz,

I A. B. do atteſt, that no part of the within-mentioned *Debt* is paid to me or my uſe, or diſcharged by me; and I do hereby Transfer the ſame to *C. D.*

The *Objections* I have met with to the making ſuch a Law are, *viz.*

Object. 1. *This would be Repugnant to our common Law, and ſome Statutes*, viz. *Maintenance, Champarty, Bankrupt*, &c.

1. I anſwer, Not ſo Repugnant as at firſt view it ſeems to be, for, though by our Laws at preſent, *Bonds* and *Bills* cannot be *Aſſigned*, *Mortgages* (which are but another kind of Security for Money lent) may be Aſſigned.

2. If any Laws at preſent are Repugnant to the common good of the Nation, and if the making of ſuch a new *Law* will effectually encreaſe the uſeful Stock of the *Nation*, at leaſt one third part, and greatly eaſe the Courſe of *Trade*, as I humbly conceive this will do, I hope none will deny but it may

conſiſt

consist with the Wisdom of *Parliament* to create new Laws.

3. Most of our Statutes were made in times before we understood Trade in *England*; and the same Policy and Laws that were good then, and may yet be good for a Country destitute of Commerce, may not be so fit for us now, nor for any Nation so abounding with Trade as *England* doth at present.

Object. 2. *May not this occasion many Cheats and Law Suits.*

Answ. 1. I answer no, Experience manifests the contrary, not only in other Kingdoms and Countries abroad where Transferrance of Bills of Debt is in use, but even in our own, where we have for many Ages had the Experience of *Indorsment on Bills of Exchange*, and in this present Age of the *passing of Gold-Smiths Notes* from one Man to another, which two practices are very like to the designed way of Transferring Bills of Debt, and yet no considerable Cheats or Inconveniencies have arisen thereby.

Answ. 2. No Man can be Cheated except it be with his own consent, and we commonly say **caveat emptor**, no Man is to be forced to accept anothers Bill that himself doth not approve of, and no Man will axcept of another Mans Bill eccept he know him, nor until he hath used means to satisfie himself concerning him, no more than he will sell his Goods to a Stranger, unless he hath some reason to believe he is able to pay him.

Object. 3. *Will not such a Law as this be very troublesom, especially in Fairs and Markets, and also to Gentlemen and Ladies, when they shall be forced for all Goods they buy above the Value of* 10*l. to give Bills under their Hands and Seals?*

I answer, this *Law* will not at all Incommode Gentlemen as to what they Buy in Shops, *&c.* neither those that converse in Fairs and Markets; for that which Gentlemen buy in Shops, *&c.* and others in Fairs, *&c.* they either pay or promise ready Money, or else say nothing of the time of payment, which the Law understands to be the same with a promise of present pay; so that if they give no Bills there is no penalty attends the neglect or refusal, but only that the contract between the Buyer and Seller shall be presumed in the Law to be as if it were made for ready Money.

CHA-

CHAP. VI.

Concerning a Court Merchant.

I Have conceived great hope from the late most Prudent and Charitable Institution of that *Judicature*, for determination of Differences touching Houses burnt by the late Fire in *London*, that this Kingdom will at length be blessed with a happy method, for the speedy, easie and cheap deciding of Differences between *Merchants Masters of Ships and Seamen*, &c. by some *Court or Courts of Merchants*, like those which are established in most of the grett Cities and Towns in *France*, *Holland* and other places; the want whereof in *England*, is and hath ever been a great bar to the Progress and Grandeur of the Trade of this Kingdom; as for instance, if *Merchants* happen to have differences with *Masters and Owners of Ships*, upon *Charter-Parties* or *Accounts* beyond Sea, &c. The

 Suit

Suit is commonly first commenced in the *Admiralty Court*, where, after tedious Attendance and vast Expences, probably just before the Cause should come to determination, it is either removed into the *Delegates*, where it may hang in suspence until the *Plaintiff* and *Defendant* have empty purses and gray Heads, or else because most Contracts for Maritim Affairs, are made upon the Land (and most Accidents happen in some Rivers or Harbours here, or beyond Sea, and not in *alto mari*) The *Defendant* brings his Writ of *Prohibition*, and removes the Cause into his *Majesties Court of King's Bench*, where, after great Expences of Time and Money, it is well if we can make our own *Council* (being *Common Lawyers*) understand one half of our Case, we being amongst them as in a Foreign Country, our Language strange to them, and theirs as strange to us; after all, no Attestations of Foreign *Notaries*, nor other publick Instruments from beyond Sea, being Evidences at Law, and the Accounts depending, consisting perhaps of an hundred or more several Articles, which are as so many Issues at Law, the Cause must come into the *Chancery*, where after many Years tedious Travels to *Westminster*, with black Boxes and green Bags, when the *Plaintiff* and *Defendant* have

tire

tired their Bodies, distracted their Minds, and consumed their Estates, the Cause, if ever it be ended, is commonly by order of that Court referred to *Merchants*, ending miserably, where it might have had at first a happy Issue; if it had begun right.

From whence follow these National Inconveniences.

1. *It is a vast Expence to the Persons concerned.*

2. *It takes off Men from following their Callings, to the Publick loss, as well as the particular Damages of the concerned, that time being lost to the Nation that is spent in Law-Suits.*

3. *It makes Men, after they have once attained indifferent Estates, to leave Trading, and for ease to turn Country Gentle-men*, whereas great and experienced Men are the only Persons that must mate the *Dutch* in Trade, if ever we do it.

4. *It is my opinion, a great cause of the Prodigality, Idleness and Injustice of many of our Masters of Ships in* England, *and consequently a wonderful bar to the growth of our* English Navigation, who knowing that their owners cannot Legally eject them, especially if the *Master* have a part of the Ship himself, but that remedy to the *Owners* will be worse than the Disease, which occasions *Masters* to presume to do those things, and be guil-

ty of ſuch neglects, as naturally they would not, if they ſtood more upon their good behaviour.

I could ſay much more of the Damage this Nation ſuſtains by the want of a *Law-Merchant*, but that is ſo evident to all Mens Experience, that I ſhall not longer inſiſt upon it, but proceed humbly to propoſe ſome particulars, which, being duely conſidered, may peradventure by wiſer Heads be Improved towards the cure of this Evil, *viz.*

1. *That it be Enacted that there ſhall be erected within the* City of London, *a ſtanding* Court Merchant, *to conſiſt of twelve able* Merchants, *ſuch as ſhall be choſen by the* Livery Men *of the ſaid City in their common Hall, at the time and in the manner herein after limited and appointed.*

2. *That the ſaid twelve perſons ſo to be Elected, or any three or more of them, ſitting at the ſame time and place, and not otherwiſe, ſhall be accounted Judiciary* Merchants, *and Authorized to hear and determine all Differences and Demands whatſoever, which have ariſen (and are not hitherto determined) or may any ways ariſe between* Merchants, Trades-Men, Artificers Maſters and Owners of Ships, Sea-Men Boat-Men and Freighters of Ships, *or any other perſon having Relation to* Merchandizing

Trad

ping, *for or concerning any Account* *f* Merchants, *Freight of Ships*, *or* *r Bills of Exchange, or Bills of* *Bumery, or for Work done upon, or* *livered to the use of any Ship, or* *sale of Goods; or any other thing* *ade or Shipping.*

y three or more of them (as the *r* did at *Clifford's-Inn*) *may pro-* *y to the hearing and determining of* *rences, and that their sentence shall* *t which there shall be no appeal or* *wise than as is hereafter mentioned,* *of Error lie for the removal, or* *same.*

y or any three of them may issue out *conveening all persons before them,* *did*, &c.

ey be a Court of Record, as the &c.

y take nothing for their own pains, *rectly, but six pence each for signing* *der in every Cause, whereof the* *oney to be paid doth not exceed* 10 *l.* *all Causes not exceeding* 100 *l.* *ach for all Causes exceeding the*

ees to be due and payable only to *any of the said Judiciary* Mer- *rd the said Cause and Causes*,

 and

and Signed the Judgments or final Decrees in them.

7. *That for Rewards to Officers, the Judiciary* Merchants *do constitute a Table of reasonable Fees, to be confirmed by the two* Lord Chief-Justices, *and* Lord Chief Baron *of the* Exchequer.

8. *That in any Case determined by a less number than seven of the said Judiciary* Merchants, *there may be an Appeal to seven or more,* as was lately practised in the afore-mentioned Judicature.

9. *That they may have power to levy Executions upon Estates real or personal, with such Restrictions as the Parliament shall please to appoint.*

10. *That the extent of the Jurisdiction of the said* Court, *shall be to all Places within ten Miles of* London, *or only to the late Lines of Communication, as the Parliament shall think fit.*

11. *That the said Judiciary* Merchants *and their Officers, before they exercise their Authority, take such Oaths as the Parliament shall please to Appoint.*

12. *That if any of the Judiciary* Merchants *be Prosecuted for exercising any of the Powers that shall be committed to them, they may plead the general Issue, and give the Act in evidence for their Defence.*

13. *That*

13. *That no Writ or Writs of* Supersedeas Certiorary, *or* Injunctions *out of any of his* Majesties Courts, *shall supersede, or stay Execution*, &c.

14. *The Act to continue* Probationarily *so long as the* Parliament *shall think fit.*

15. *That the twelve Judiciary* Merchants *shall be chosen Yearly by all the Free-men that are Livery-men of* London, *in the* Guild Hall *of the said* City, *or by so many of them as shall be present at such Elections, upon every* Munday, *Yearly, next before the Feast day of* St. Michael (or as the Parliament shall appoint) *in manner following;* Every *Livery-man then present, to deliver unto any two such* Aldermen, *and four* Commoners, *as the* Lord Mayor *and* Court of Aldermen *for the time being, shall appoint to take the view or scrutiny of Election, a Paper containing the names of such twelve Persons as he thinks best to be Elected for the purposes aforesaid, setting his, the said Electors, own name on the back-side of the said Paper; and the next* Munday *after, in the said* Guild-Hall, *the said two* Aldermen, *and four* Commoners, *or so many of them as shall have taken the Scrutiny, shall publickly declare unto the* Lord Mayor, Aldermen, *and* Commoners *then present, who are the twelve Persons chosen by the majority of Votes, and how many Votes each of them had.*

16. *If it happen that any of the Judiciary* Mer-

Merchants *dye before the end of the Year, or refuse to undertake the Trust, it be lawful for the Livery-men to choose another or others toties quoties. And the Lord Mayor be enjoyned to summon Common-Halls to that purpose.*

17. *That every Year six of the old Judiciary* Merchants *go off in course, and be uncapable of being re-elected, and six new ones chose in their stead,* viz. *All the twelve to be re-chosen, but only six of the old ones that had the most Voices to hold next Year, altho' more of them should happen to be Elected for the next Year.*

Object. 1. The main *Objections* that I can fore-see will be made against this Constitution, is, that *It thwarts that most excellent order of our English Juries.*

Answ. 1. I answer, that I hope there is no *English-man* more in love with *Juries* than my self; but it is evident that the common way of Tryals, doth not well reach the variety and strangeness of *Merchants* cases, especially in relation to foreign Affairs.

Answ. 2. What better Jury can a *Merchant* hope for, than twelve able and honest *Merchants*, chose by the collective Body of the whole City, and such as shall all of them stand upon their Good Behaviour to be turned out with Ignominy the next Year, if they do not equal right to all Men.

Object.

Object. 2. *The admitting of no Appeals from a Court-Merchant seems too arbitrary.*

I answer; While we choose our *Judges* our selves for Merchants cases, and may remove them our selves, in my opinion they can be no more too Arbitrary than too much Power can be given to Referees, when both parties desire an end of their Differences; besides, if their Power be not great, the main designs of cheap, speedy, and short issues will be lost. But if it shall please the *Parliament*, there may be in the Act an appeal reserved to the House of Lords, the Money condemned to be first paid or deposited before the Appeal be allowed.

CHAP.

CHAP. VII.

Concerning Naturalization.

THat an Act of *Naturalization* of Strangers would tend to the advancement of Trade, and encrease of the value of Lands of this Kingdom, is now so generally owned and assented to, by all degrees of Men amongst us, that I doubt not but a short time will produce some *Act* or *Acts* of *Parliament* to that purpose.

I have therefore thought it not impertinent to note some few Particulars, which, if not warily prevented, may deprive us of the greatest part of the Fruit hoped for by so good a design, *viz.*

1*st*, *The Priviledges of incorporated Cities and Towns.*

2*dly*, *More especially the Societies of Artificers and Trades-men belonging to some Cities, and Towns Corporate, such as Weavers, Coopers, and many others who by vertue of their Charters pretend to priviledge and Jurisdiction, not only*

to

to the utmost extent of the Liberties of their respective Cities and Towns, but to the distance of ten miles about them.

3. *That branch of the Statute of* 5th *of* Elizabeth, *which enacts, that none shall use any manual Occupation that hath not served an Apprentiship thereunto, upon which Statute it hath been usual to Indict Strangers work-men that have exercised their Callings in the out-parts of* London.

Upon this point of *Naturalization*, many Men make a great doubt whether it be for publick Good to permit the *Jews* to be Naturalized in common with other Strangers.

Those that are against their admission, who for the most part are Merchants, urge these Reasons.

1. They say the *Jews* are a subtil People, prying into all kind of Trades, and thereby depriving the *English* Merchant of that profit he would otherwise gain.

2. They are a penurious People, living miserably, and therefore can, and do, afford to trade for less profit than the *English*, to the prejudice of the *English* Merchant.

3. They bring no Estates with them, but set up with their Pens and Ink only; and if after some few Years they thrive and grow rich, they carry away their Riches with them to some other Country (being

a

a People that cannot mix with us) which Riches being carried away, is a publick loss to this Kingdom.

Those that are for the admission of the *Jews*, say in answer to the aforesaid Reasons, *viz.*

1*st*, The subtiller the *Jews* are, and the more Trades they pry into while they live here, the more they are like to encrease Trade; and the more they do that, the better it is for the Kingdom in general, though the worse for the *English* Merchant, who comparatively to the rest of the People of *England* is not one of a thousand.

2*dly*, The thriftier they live, the better Example to our People; *there being nothing in the World more conducing to enrich a Kingdom than thriftiness.*

3*dly*, It is denyed that they bring over nothing with them; for many have brought hither very good Estates, and hundreds more would do the like, and settle here for their Lives, and their Posterities after them, if they had the same freedom and Security here as they have in *Holland* and *Italy*, where the *Grand Duke of Tuscany*, and other Princes allow them not only perfect Liberty and Security, but give them the priviledge of making Laws among themselves; and that they would reside with us, is proved from

the

the known Principles of Nature, *viz.*

Principle 1. *All Men by Nature are alike, as I have before demonstrated, and* Mr. Hobbs *hath truly asserted, how Erroneous soever he may be in other things.*

Principle 2. *Fear is the cause of Hatred, and hatred of separation from, as well as evil Deeds to, the Parties or Government hated, when opportunity is offer'd: This by the way shews the difference between a bare connivance at Dissenters in matters of Religion, and a tolleration by Law; the former keeps them continually in Fear, and consequently apt to Sedition and Rebellion, when any probable occasion of success presents: The latter disarms cunning, ambitious minded Men, who, wanting a popular discontented Party to work upon, can effect little or nothing to the prejudice of the Government. And this methinks discovers clearly the cause why the* Lutherans *in* Germany, Protestants in France, Greeks in Turkey, and Sectaries in Holland, *are such quiet peaceable-minded-men, while our* Non-conformists in England *are said to be enclined to strife, War, and Bloodshed;* **Take away the Cause and the Effect will cease.**

While the Laws are in Force against Men, they think the Sword hangs over their Heads, and are always in fear (though the Execution be suspended) *not knowing how soon Councils, or Counsellors, Times or Persons, may change,* it is only

only **Perfect Love that casts out Fear**; and all Men are in love with *Liberty* and Security: It cannot be denyed that the Industrious *Bees* have Stings (tho' Drones have not) yet *Bees sting not, except those that hurt them, or disturb their Hives.*

It is said, the *Jews* cannot Intermarry with us, and therefore it cannot be supposed they will reside long amongst us, altho' they were treated never so kindly: Why not reside here as well as in *Italy*, *Poland*, and *Holland*? They have now no Country of their own to go to, and therefore that is their Country, and must needs so esteemed by them, where they are best used, and have the greatest Security.

CHAP. VIII.

Concerning Wool and Woolen Manufactuers.

THat *Wool* is eminently the Foundation of the *English* Riches, I have not heard lenied by any, and that therefore all possible neans ought to be used to keep it within our wn *Kingdom*, is generally confessed; and to his purpose most of our modern *Parliaments* ave strenously endeavoured the contriving f severe *Laws* to prevent its Exportation, nd the last *Act* made it *Felony* to Ship out *Wool*, *Woolfels*, &c.

Notwithstanding which, we see that *English and Irish Wool* goes over so plentifully, hat it is within a very small matter as cheap Holland as in *England*.

The means to prevent this Evil, by additional *Penal Laws*, and alterations of some those now in being, were long under ebate, by his *Majesties* command, in the ouncil *of Trade*, who, according to their duty, took great pains therein; and since, I have been informed, the same things were under Consideration in *Parliament*, so that I doubt not, but in due time we shall see some more effectual Laws enacted to this purpose, as well in relation to *Ireland* (from whence the greatest of this mischief proceeds) as in *England*, than ever yet have been; yet I do utterly dispair of ever seeing this Disease perfectly cured, till the Causes thereof be removed, which I take to be;

1st. *Heighth of Interest in* England, which an Abatement by a Law to 4 *per cent* would Cure.

2dly, *Want of Hands*, which an Act of Naturalization would Cure.

3dly, *Compulsion in matters of Religion*, which some Relaxation of the *Ecclesiastical* Laws, I hope, would effectually Cure.

For while our Neighbours, through the cheap Valuation of their Stocks, can afford to Trade, and disburse their Money for less Profit than we, as hath been, I think, sufficiently Demonstrated by the foregoing Discourse, and have more Hands to employ than we, by reason of the large Immunities and Priviledges they give both to Natives and Foreigners, there is no question but they will be able to give a better Price for our *Wool*, than we can afford our selves; and they

they that can give the best Price for a Commodity shall never fail to have it, by one means or other, notwithstanding the *opposition* of any *Laws*, or *interposition* of any *Power* by Sea or Land; of such force, subtilty and violence is the general Course of Trade.

Object. But some may say, and take it as well from what I have writ elsewhere, as from their own Observations; Will not the well-making of our *Woolen Manufactures*, contribute much to the keeping of our *Wool* naturally within our own Kingdom?

I answer, Doubtless it will have a great tendency thereunto, but can never effect it, till the aforesaid Radical Causes of this Disease be removed, which brings me to the next Question, *viz.*

What will Improve our Woolen Manufacturies in Quality and Quantity?

This is a very great Question, and requires very deliberate and serious Consideration, but I shall write my present Thoughts concerning it, desiring those *Gentlemen*'s Pardon, from whom I may differ in Opinion, having this to say for my self, that I do it not rashly, this being a Business that I have many Years considered of, and that not solitarily, but upon converse with the most skilful Men in our several *English Woolen* Manufactures.

1. Then I say, *Those three fore-mentioned Particulars which will naturally keep our Wool at home, will as naturally encrease our Woolen Manufactures.*

2. Negatively, *I think that very few of our Laws now in force to this purpose* (though our Statute Books are replenished with many) *have any tendency thereunto, nor any thing I have yet seen in Print*; For,

1st, All our *Laws*, relating to the *Aulnegers* Duty, every Body knows, signifie nothing to the encrease or well-making our *Manufactures*, but are rather Chargeable and Prejudicial.

2dly, All our *Laws* that oblige our People to the making of Strong, Substantial (and as we call it, *Loyal*) Cloath, of a certain length, breadth and weight, if they were duly put in Execution, would in my *Opinion* do more hurt than good, because the Humors and Fashions of the *World* change, and at some times in some places (as now in most) slight, cheap, light *Cloath* will sell more plentifully and better than that which is heavier, stronger, and truer wrought; and *If we intend to have the Trade of the World, we must imitate the* Dutch, *who make the worst as well as the best of all Manufactures, that we may be in a capacity of serving all* Markets *and all* Humors.

3dly

3*dly*, I conclude all our *Laws* limiting the umbers of *Loomes* numbered, or kind of *ervants*, and times of Working, to be cerainly Prejudicial to the Cloathing of the Kingdom in general, though they be adantagious to some particular Men or Places, who first procured those Laws of Restriction and Limitation.

4*thly*, I think all those Laws are Prejudicial, that prohibit a *Weaver* from being a *Fuller*, *Tucker* or *Dyer*, or a *Fuller* or *Tucker* from keeping a *Loome*.

5*thly*, I conclude that stretching of *Cloath* by *Tentors*, tho' it be sometimes prejudicial to the Cloath, is yet absolutely necessary to the Trade of *England*, and that the excess of Straining cannot be certainly limited by any Law, but must be left to the Seller's or Exporter's Discretion, who best knows what will please his Customers beyond the Seas; besides, if we would wholly prohibit *straining of Cloath*, the *Dutch* (as they have often done) would buy our unstrain'd *Cloath*, and carry it into *Holland*, and there strain it to six or seven Yards *per* Piece more in length, and make it look a little better to the Eye, and after that carry it abroad to *Turkey*, and other Markets, and there beat us out of Trade with our own Weapons.

But some may then ask me, Whether I

think it would be for the advantage of the Trade of *England*, to leave all Men at liberty to make what *Cloath* and *Stuff* they please, how they will, where and when they will, of any lengths or sizes?

I answer; *Yes*, certainly in my Judgment it would be so, except such Species only as his *Majesty* and the *Parliament* shall think fit to make *Staples*, as suppose *Colchester Bayes*, *Perpetuanoes*, *Cheanyes*, and some other sorts of *Norwitch Stuffs*, to be allowed the honour of a *publick Seal*, by which to be Bought and Sold here, and beyond *Seas*, as if it were upon the publick Faith of *England*; and wherever such Seal is allowed, or shall be thought fit to be affixed on any Commodity, I would desire the Commodity should be exactly made according to the Institution, and always kept to its certain length, breadth and goodness.

But in case any should make of the said Commodities worse than the Institution, I think it would be most for the publick advantage to impose no penalty upon them, but only deny them the Benefit and reputation of the publick Seal, to such *Bayes* or *Stuffs* as shall be insufficient; which in my opinion would be punishment enough to those that should make worse than the Standard, and advantage enough to those that should keep to it.

2. For

2. For all *Cloaths* and *Stuffs* not being made *Staples*, I think it would be of very great uſe that the makers did Weave in their Marks, and affix their own Seals, containing the length and breadth of the Pieces (as hath been provided in ſome Statutes) and that no Maker under ſevere Penalties ſhall uſe another Mark or Seal, with ſuch Penalty to every Maker or Seller, whoſe *Cloath* or *Stuffs* ſhall not contain the length and breadth ſet upon the Seal, as his *Majeſty* and the *Parliament* ſhall think fit.

3. If the Makers of all Stuffs whatſoever for Exportation, whether *Staples* or not (which are commonly ſold by the Piece, and not by the Yard or Ell) were obliged to make them no ſhorter than anciently they have been made; the particular lengths of each ſort whereof might be provided for, and expreſſed in the *Act*; this good effect would follow upon it, *viz.*

At all *Foreign Markets*, where we pay a great *Cuſtom* by the Piece, according to the Book of Rates, currant in the ſeveral Countries, we ſhould pay but the ſame Cuſtom abroad for a Piece of full length which now we do for one that is ſhorter: Notwithſtanding, I conceive it would be expedient to leave it to the Makers diſcretion, to make their Pieces as much longer as they pleaſe.

CHAP. IX.

Concerning the Ballance of TRADE.

THat the greatness of this *Kingdom* depends upon Foreign Trade, is generally acknowledged, and therefore the Interest of Trade not unbecoming Persons of the highest Rank; and of this Study as well as others, it may be said, there's an infinity in it, none, though of the largest Intellects and Experience, being able to fathom its utmost depth.

Among other things relating to Trade, there hath been much discoursed of the Ballance of Trade; the right understanding whereof may be of singular use, and serve as a Compass to stear by, in the Contemplations and Propagation of Trade for publick advantage.

The Ballance of Trade is commonly understood two ways.

1. Gene-

1. Generally, *Something whereby it may be known whether this Kingdom gaineth or loseth by Foreign Trade.*

2. Particularly, *Something whereby we may know by what Trades this Kingdom gains, and by what Trades it loseth.*

For the first of these,

It is the most general received Opinion, and that not ill grounded, that this *Ballance* is to be taken by a strict Scrutiny of what Proportion the value of the Commodities exported out of this *Kingdom* bear to those Imported; *and if the Exports exceed the Imports*, it is concluded the *Nation* gets by the general course of its Trade, it being supposed that the over-pluss is Imported in *Bullion*, and so adds to the Treasure of the Kingdom; *Gold and Silver being taken for the measure and standard of Riches.*

2. This Rule is not only commonly applied to the general course of Foreign *Trade*, but to particular Trades to and from this Nation to any other.

Now, although this Notion have much of Truth in it, and was ingeniously and worthily started by him that first Published it; and much good hath accrued to the Kingdom by our Law-makers (*Noblemen* and *Gentlemen*) resenting it, yet if the difficulty of the Scrutiny whereby to reduce it into practice,

practice, and the many Accidents that may accrue, be seriously weighed, it will appear too doubtful and uncertain as to our general *Trade*, and in reference to particular *Trades* Fallible and Erroneous.

That it will not hold as to Foreign Trade in general, appears,

1. From the difficulty and impossibility of taking a true account, as well of the quantity, as of the value of Commodities Exported and Imported.

The general rule for this hath been the *Custom-House-Books*, but that they cannot be in any measure certain will easily be granted: For,

1. As to the quantity, if it be considered that many fine Commodities of small Bulk and great Value, as *Points*, *Laces*, *Ribands*, *fine Linnen*, *Silks*, *Jewels*, &c. are Imported by stealth; and that also in many *Out-Ports* and *Creeks* of *England* and *Wales*, Commodities of Bulk are both Imported and Exported often times by indirect means, that never are *Registred*; besides also of what is entered, there may be (though not considerable in *London*) yet, in other parts much difference in the quantities and qualities.

2. As to the value, how shall the compute be made, seeing the Rates of the *Customs* are in no kind proportionable, our own Commodities

modities being ſome rated very low, as *Drapery*, *Silk-Wares*, *Haberdaſhery*, and all *Manufactures* of *Iron*; others high, as *Lead* and *Tin*; and *Fiſh* in *Engliſh* Shipping nothing; and for Foreign *Commodities* Imported, the Rates are yet more unequal, ſo that the value Rated for the *Cuſtoms* cannot be a due meaſure.

Beſides, Foreign *Commodities* Imported by *Engliſh* Shipping, ſhould be valued only at their firſt Coſt and Charges abroad, and thoſe by Foreign Shipping, with the encreaſe of the home-ward *Freight*.

2. From the many Accidents that fall out in *Trade*, without the true knowledge whereof a right *Ballnace* cannot be made, as,

1 Accidents that diminiſh the Stock ſent out, as loſſes at Sea, bad Markets, Bankrupts, alſo Confiſcations, Sieſures and Arreſts, which fall out often on ſeveral occaſions.

Now, if by any of theſe, or ſuch like, the original Stock comes to be impaired, and leſſened, the value of the *Commodities* Imported in return, may be far leſs than the value of the *Commodities* Exported, and yet may be the full product, and ſo the Nation no Gainer, though the Exports were more in value than the Imports.

2. Accidents whereby the Stock ſent out, comes to be extraordinarily advanced in Sale abroad,

abroad, from whence it may fall out, that the Commodities Imported in return, may appear to be of a much greater value than the Commodities Exported, and yet be no more than the real produce of them, and so the Nation no loser, but a gainer thereby, although the Imports exceeds the Exports.

And if the afore-cited Instances suffice not to prove the uncertainty (in some cases) of this Notion, of the Ballance of Trade, the following Examples of *Ireland*, *Virginia* and *Barbadoes*, are so pregnant to this Case, as, I think, will convince any Man: For those three Countries do without doubt Export Annually a far greater value of the Commodities of their native growth and product, than is imported to them from hence, or from any Foreign Country, and yet they are not such great Gainers, but continue Poor; the true reason whereof, as to *Ireland*, is given by the most Ingenious *Author* of that *Treatise of Taxes and Contributions*, Page 27. where he saith, *That a great part of Estates both real and personal in* Ireland, *are owned by Absentees, and such as draw over the Profits raised out of* Ireland, *refunding nothing*; so as *Ireland* Exporting more than it Imports, doth yet grow poorer to a Paradox.

Here let me glaunce at my old Theme, and

and desire the *Reader* to consider seriously, whether it may, not improperly, be said of all Kingdoms and Countries, where the *Interest of Money* runs higher than their Neighbours, that a part of their Estates are owned by *Absentees*, and consequently they shall be sure to be kept Poor, whether their Importations or their Exportations exceed.

This likewise resolves a Question that was once put to me by an *Honourable Person* concerning the *County of Cornwell*, which notwithstanding the great quantity of *Tin* and *Pilchards*, which Annually the *Inhabitants* are sending forth from their two *Mines* of Land and Sea, yet the *Country* still remains in a poor Condition; *The reason* whereof to me seems clearly to be, *Because a great part of the Stock imployed in the aforesaid great Trade, is taken up at Interest, and consequently owned by* Londoners, *and other* Absentees.

And though it may be hoped that this is not yet the case of *England*, yet it is a Demonstration that the notion of taking the **Ballance** this way, is not absolutely, and in all places, and under all circumstances, without exception true and good; for in case the Trade of *England* should be carried on by *Absentees*, then the supposition upon which this Notion is grounded (*viz.* That when the Exports Over-*Ballance* the Imports, the

Sur-

Surplusage is returned into *England* in *Bullion*) will prove a mistake, and the contrary will be true, *viz*. That the Surplusage will be conveighed into Foreign Parts, to the places of the residence of such *Absentees*.

2. The second thing I am to Illustrate is, that this Rule (barely considered) is Fallible and Erroneous, as to particular and distinct Trades.

This will appear, if it be considered, that a true measure of any particular Trade, as to the profit or loss of the Nation thereby, cannot be taken by the consideration of such Trade in it self singly, but as it stands in reference, and is subservient to the general Trade of the Kingdom; for it may so fall out, that there may be some places to which little of our *English Manufactures* are Exported, and yet the Commodities we have from thence, may be so necessary to the carrying on our Trade in general, or some other particular Trades, that without them the Nation would greatly decline and decay in Trade.

Now, in this case, if we should measure such a particular Trade by the aforesaid Notion of the Ballance, we should find the Imports abundantly exceed the Exports, and so be ready to conclude against such a Trade as destructive, whereas (notwithstanding) it

may

may, in truth, be a very neceſſary beneficial Trade, and to the very great advantage of the Nation; as for inſtance,

The Trade of *Denmark* and *Norway*, the *Imports* from whence are certainly many times the value of our Native Commodities Exported thither, and yet it cannot be denied but that Trade is advantagious to the Kingdom, not only becauſe it gives, or would give employments to two Hundred, or three Hundred Sail of *Engliſh* Shipping (*if we did a little mend our Act of Navigation*) but principally becauſe the Commodities imported from thence, as *Timber*, *Pitch*, *Deals* and *Tar*, are of ſuch neceſſary uſe, in order to the building and ſupplying our Shipping, that without them other Trades could not be carried on.

It will not be denied by the Honourable *Eaſt-India Company*, but they import much more *Goods* into *England*, than they export, and that, to purchaſe the ſame, they carry out quantities of Gold and Silver annually; yet no Man that underſtands any thing of the Trade of the World, will affirm, that *England* loſeth by that Trade. The *Dutch*, with good reaſon, eſteem the Trade of the *Eaſt-Indies* more Profitable to them than are the Mines of Gold and Silver in *America* to the *King* of *Spain*; and if the *Engliſh Companies*

were

were vested by Act of Parliament with so much *Authority* as the *Dutch* have, and thereby encouraged to drive as full a Trade thither, as the *Dutch* do, I doubt not but it would be so (not so much to the private gain of the Members of that Company, as) to the publick Profit of this Kingdom in general; however, as it is, it will not be difficult to prove that it is the most beneficial Trade this Nation drives at present; For,

1*st*, That Trade constantly employs 25 to 30 Sail of the most War-like Ships in *England*, with Sixty to a Hundred Men in each Ship, and may in two or three Years more employ a greater Number; and in order to the carrying on that Trade, that *Company* hath lately (unconstrained) given considerable *Encouragements* for the Building of great Ships, which hath had good effect.

2*dly*, It supplies the Nation constantly and fully, with that (in this Age) necessary material of *Salt-Petre*.

3*dly*, It employs the Nation, for its Consumption, with *Pepper*, *Indico*, *Callicoes*, and several useful *Drugs*, near the value of 150000 *Pound* to 180000 *Pound* per annum.

4*thly*, It furnisheth us with *Pepper*, *Cowryes*, *Long-Cloath*, *and other Callicoes* and *painted Stuffs*, proper for the Trade of *Turkey*, *Italy*, *Spain*, *France* and *Guiny*, to the amount of f 2 or 300000 *l. per Annum*; most of which 'rades we could not carry on with any conlerable advantage, but for those supplies; id *these Goods exported do produce in foreign rts, to be returned to* England, *six times the reasure in Specie, that the Company exports om hence.*

Now, if not only the aforesaid advanta:s be seriously considered, but also what :triment the *Nation* would sustain, if we ere deprived of those supplies, both in)int of Strength and War-like Provisions, regard of Shiping and *Salt-Petre*, but also respect of the furtherance it gives to ma/ other Trades before-mentioned, it will sily appear that this Trade, tho' its Im)rts exceeds its Exports, is the most adntagious Trade to *England*, and deserves l encouragement; for were we to buy all ır *Pepper* and *Callicoes*, &c. of the *Dutch*, ey would raise our *Pepper* (*which now stands ? Nation but about* 3 *d. per pound in India*) to, near, the proportion which they have adnced on *Nutmegs*, *Cloves* and *Mace* (which st the *Dutch* not much morh *per pound* in *dia* than *Pepper*) since they engrossed the :ade for those Commodities; and the use *Callicoes* in *England* would be supplyed by 'eign Linnen at greater Prices; so that ıat may be secured from this Nation's con-

O sumption,

ſumption, would in probability coſt then above 400000 *l. per Annum* more than nov it doth; and our foreign Trades, for *Italy* *Guiny*, &c. would in part decay for want c the aforeſaid ſupplies.

There is another Notion concerning th *Ballance of Trade*, which I think not Imper tinent here to take notice of, *viz.* Some ar of opinion, that the way to know wheth the *Nation* getteh or looſeth in the gener by its foregoing Trade, is to take an inſp ction into the courſe of the *Exchange*; if g nerally above the intrinſick value or *Par* the *Coins* of Foreign Countries, we not on looſe by ſuch *Exchanges*, but the ſame is demonſtration that we looſe by the gener courſe of our foreign Trade; and that w require more ſupply of Commodities fro abroad, than our exports in Goods do ſer to purchaſe: And certain it is, that wh once the *Exchange* comes to be 5 or 6 *per c* above the true value of foreign Monies, o Treaſure would be carried out, whatev Laws ſhould be made to prevent it: And the contrary, when the *Exchange* is genera below the true value of our foreign *Coins*, i an evidence that our exports do in value ceed what we require from abroad: And if the *Exchange* comes to be 5 or 6 *per c* below the true value of the foreign Coi

rett

turns will be made for *England* in the
oins of foreign Countries.

Now, that there is also a great deal of
ruth in this Notion, is not to be denied,
d that the diligent observance and consi-
ration of the course of the Exchange, may
of use and very necessary in many respects,
d is a very Ingenious Study for any that
ould dive into the Mysteries of Trade; yet,
cause this is likewise subject to vary on
any Accidents and Emergencies of State
d War, *&c.* and because there is no settled
ourse of *Exchange*, but to and from *France*,
olland, *Flanders*, *Hambrough*, *Venice*, *Leghorn*
d *Genoa*, and that there are many other
reat and eminent Trades, besides what are
riven to those Countries, this cannot afford
true and satisfactory *solution* to the present
uestion.

Thus having demonstrated that these No-
ons, touching the Ballance of Trade, tho'
ey are in their kind useful Notions, are in
me cases fallible and uncertain. If any shall
k, *How shall we then come to be resolved of the
atter in Question.*

I answer, *First*, The best and most certain
iscovery, to my apprehension, is to be made
om the encrease or diminution of our
rade aud *Shipping* in general; for if our Trade
d Shipping diminish, whatever profit par-

 ticular

ticular Men may make, the *Nation* undoubt edly loseth; and on the contrary, *if our Trac and Shipping encrease*, how small or low soeve the profits are to private Men, it is an infa lible Indication that the Nation in gener thrives; for I dare affirm, and that Categor cally, in all parts of the whole World, wher ever Trade is great, and continues so ar grows daily more great, and encreaseth Shipping, and that for a succession not of few Years, but of Ages, that Trade must Nationally profitable.

As a Town where only a Fair is kept, every Year the number of People and Com modities do augment, that Town, howev the Markets are, will gain; whereas there come still fewer and fewer People a Commodities, that place will decline a decay. Discoursing once with a *Noble L* concerning this measure or method of kno ing the *Ballance of our Trade*, or more plai our general *National* gain or loss by *Tra* his *Lordship* was pleased to oppose, by ask two very proper Questions, *viz.*

Quest. 1. *Is there not a great similitude twcen the Affairs of a private Person, and a Nation, the former being but a little Family, the latter a great Family?*

I answer, Yes; certainly there is.

Quest. 2. His *Lordships* second Quest

as, *May not a private Merchant be, or seem be owner of much Shipping, drive a great Trade, ceive and send out many Goods, and yet decline d grow poorer, notwithstanding all his umbling d busseling?*

I answer; Yes, certainly he may; but this ill soon appear, either while he lives, or at s Death; and his great Trade will come be but a small one, or none at all: But that an who drives a great Trade, and is owner employer of much Shipping, and doth all s dayes continue and encrease in Trade nd Shipping, and his Son or Successor after m, and after him his Grand-Son, *&c.* this ould be an indisputable Evidence that that erson or Family did thrive by their Trade; r if they had not thriven, their Trade ould not have long continued, much less creased: This is the case of Nations, and is through God's Goodness is the case of *ngland* (as bad as we are at present.)

The reason of this is as evident as the first, r *where a great Trade is driven,* especially here much Shipping is employed, whatever comes of the poor *Merchant,* that drives e Trade, *Multitudes of People will be certain iners,* as his *Majesty* and his *Officers of Cu-m,* besides *Shipwrights, Butchers, Brewers, kers, Rope-makers, Porters, Sea men, Manu-cturers, Carmen, Lighter-men, and all other*

Artificers and People that depend on Trade and Shipping; which indeed more or leſs the whole Kingdom doth.

But it may be ſaid again, *If this encreaſe of Trade depend upon, and proceed from our ordinary Importations, for which our ready Money goes out, it will impoveriſh us.*

I anſwer, in ſome caſes it may be ſo, and in ſome caſes (as I have already demonſtrated) it may be otherwiſe, but that will best be known by the effects; for if we are impoveriſhed, our general Trade and our Shipping will neceſſarily and viſibly grow leſs and leſs, and muſt rationally and unavoidably do ſo; for that being impoveriſhed, we ſhall loſe our Tools (our Stock) to drive a great Trade with; whereas on the contrary, if our Trade in the groſs bulk of it (tho' we may decline in ſome) do ſtill encreaſe, eſpecially our Shipping for a long tract of Years, it is infallible proof of our thriving by our Trade, and that we are ſtill getting more Tools (more Stock) to Trade with.

Some there are would limit this diſcovery to the encreaſe and diminution of our Coin and Bullion, but, becauſe that is more ſecret and indiſcernable, it cannot, I conceive, afford ſo clear a demonſtration as the other, if any at all; for that Money ſeems to vulgar

Obſ

Obſervers moſt plentiful when there is leaſt occaſion for it; and on the contrary, more ſcarce, as the occaſions for the employment thereof are more numerous and advantagious, according to which we ſhould ſeem to have moſt Money when we have the leaſt Trade, and yet then certainly the *Nation* gets leaſt. This is apparent to thoſe that will obſerve, that when the *Eaſt-India-Company* have a great ſale to make, then Money is generally found to be ſcarce in *London*, not that it is ſo in reality more than at other times, but becauſe that extraordinary occaſion engageth Men to employ quantities, which they provide and lay aſide for that purpoſe; from the ſame reaſon it is, that a high rate of Uſury makes Money ſeem ſcarce, becauſe every Man then, as ſoon as he can take up a ſmall ſum, ſends it into the *Goldſmiths*, whereof more is ſaid before in the Preface to this Diſcourſe.

I anſwer, that tho' the Study of the *Ballance of Trade* in this laſt mentioned reſpect be a Study very Ingenious and Commendable, yet, in my poor Opinion, the enquiry, whether we get or loſe, doth not ſo much deſerve our greateſt pains and care, as how we may be ſure to get, the former being of no uſe but in order to the latter; and this therefore leads to the conſideration of the *other Ballance of Trade*, as most useful and necessary, *viz.*

What is to be done in England *to improve the Trade thereof to such a degree as to equalize or over-ballance our Neighbours in our National Profit by our Foreign Trade?*

I answer, this is a large and extensive Question, and requires to resolve it, the greatest Skill and Experience both in affairs of State and Trade, and therefore I have only made an Essay towards it, which the whole Discourse foregoing is (and therefore I hope the Reader will accept of my good affection to my Country herein, tho' he meet not with that full satisfaction he might expect and wish for.)

The method I propose for the further answering of this great Question, is (following my own principle, that if Trade be great, and much *English Shipping* employed, it will be good for the *Nation* in general, whatever it may be for private *Merchants*) First to lay down some general Rules for the enlargement of *Trade* in *England*; and then some ways of reducing those general Rules into Use and Practice. The general Rules for the enlargement of Trade are not many.

1. *Encrease Hands* } *in Trade.*
2. *Encrease Stock* }

3. *Make Trade easie and necessary*, i. e. *make it our Interest to Trade.*

4. *Make it the Interest of other Nations to Trade with us.*

1. *To encrease Hands in Trade*, the following Particulars would much contribute.

1st. *An Act of Naturalization* before mentioned.

2. *Some enlargement of the Foundations of Societies of Merchants*, as before-limited.

3. *A more easie and free admission of Inhabitants, Merchants, and Artificers, to be Burgers of our Cities and Bouroughs.*

4. *Not to hinder any Man from keeping as many Servants as he can, nor Looms, working-Tools*, &c.

5. *To abate the Interest of Money*, as aforesaid.

6. *Some Relaxations of the Ecclesiastical Laws, would keep our own People at Home, and invite others to us*, and consequently encrease the number of our Hands in Trade.

7. *Employ, Educate and Relieve the Poor, so as they may neither be Idle, nor perish for want, or leave the Land by Reason of their Miserie.*

8. *Giving such Honour and Preferment to Merchants in the Affairs of the Nation, as their Experience and Education hath fitted them for, will doubtless encrease the number.*

To encrease our Stock in Trade.

1. All the ſix fore-going particulars, will very much contribute, eſpecially the Abatement of Intereſt, becauſe bringing in of more Stock, for that the Perſons engaged in Trade, muſt neceſſarily bring in their Stocks with them, if they have any; and for Artificers that have none, their Labour in conſequence will generate Stock to the Nation, and encreaſe that we have already.

2. A Law for *Transferrance of Bills of Debt*, (as before-mentioned) will much and ſpeedily augment our uſeful Stock.

3. *The reſtraining of the Trades of our own Plantations wholly to England*, and preventing all kinds of abuſes of that part of the *Acts of Trade and Navigation*, would tend much to the encreaſe of our Stock in Trade.

4. *The ſecuring of that great Trade for Shiping imployed for importation of Timber, Maſts, Boards and Pipe-Staves*, into theſe three Kingdoms, to be done only by his *Majeſtie's* Subjects, and not by any Strangers, would in a very few Years much encreaſe the Stock of *England*.

5. *Prevention of the exportation of our Wool*, and encourageing our *Woollen Manufactures*.

6. *Encourage and Encreaſe our Fiſhing Trades*, which, how that is only to be done, is before-mentioned.

7. *To set up the* Linnen *rather than the* Woolen *Manufacture in* Ireland, and give extraordinary encouragement and priviledges to the first Undertakers.

8. *To encourage those Trades most, that vend most of our Manufactures, or supply us with Materials to be further Manufactured in* England, or else such as furnish us with Commodities for the carrying on of other Trades, as the *East-India-Company* doth eminently.

9. *If his* Majesties *Navy, Debts,* &c. *were all paid, and if for the future all his* Majesties *Payments were made with punctuality, it would much increase the Stock of this Nation in Trade;* such fatal stops being to the Body politick, like great obstructions of the Liver and Spleen to the Body Natural, which not only procure ill habits, but sometimes desperate and acute Diseases, as well as Chronical.

10. *Lessening the number of our Holy-days would encrease the days of our working, and working more would make us Richer:* Riches and Stock are the same.

11. *If our Affairs would permit, that the full Custom should be paid back,* &c. *(and not the half only) for all foreign Goods brought hither, and afterwards Exported* (as I am credibly informed the *French King* hath very lately done in all the parts of his Dominions) *it would wonderfully encrease our Navigation,* and in

in consequence our People, as well as our Domestick and Foreign Trade; and in my opinion be much better for the Nation in general, than particular free Ports.

And if only such foreign Goods as should be Loaden outwards on *English* Shiping, had the benefit of this Indulgence, it would be much the more Efficacious as to our main concern, *viz.* the encrease and improvement of our *English Navigation.*

3*d.* General Rule, *To make Trade easie and necessary*, and thereby to make it our Interest to Trade.

1. To make Trade easie, *a Law for Transferrance of Bills of Debt, will do much* (as before.)

2. *To make Trade easie, a Court-Merchant will do much* (as before in that Chapter.)

3. *Taking of the Burden of Trade, whereof one is, the great trouble and delays in receiveing back our impost at the Custom-House, and the great Charge of Fees to Searchers, Waiters*, &c.

4. *Reducing Interest of Money to* 4 per cent, will make Trade easie to the Borrowers, and to make it necessary it is the Unum Magnum (as before is said) for while we that are *Merchants*, can so easily turn *Gentlemen* by buying Lands for less then twenty Years purchase, let no Man expect that, if we thrive, we will drudge all our dayes in Trade;

Trade; or if we would, to be ſure our Sons will not.

5. To make Trade eaſie, and Wool riſe, which is always aimed at by our Parliaments; Nothing will conduce ſo much in times of War, as to appoint ſufficient regular Convoys to Merchant Ships, which ſometimes have been forced to lie full Loaden with Draperies Five or Six Months in the River for want of Convoys, with the Intereſt of 6 *per cent* eating upon them; while likewiſe their Cloath by long lying in the Ships is much damnified, and Merchants cannot buy more of the Cloathiers until their Goods are at their ſelling Ports, which when there arrived Merchants can value themſelves upon them by Exchange, and begin a freſh Inveſtment in *England*,

6. To make Trade eaſie, ſome abatement of that rigorous way of Preſſing Sea-men, which ſometimes ſweeps away the Officers as well as common men, would much conduce, it being an inſuperable diſcouragement to Merchants to have their Ships ſometimes manned, and unmanned, two or three times in a Voyage, before they can get them clear into the Sea, which is not ſo in *Holland*.

4th. General Rule, *To make it the Intereſt of other Nations to Trade with us.*

1. Being in a good condition of Strength

at

at home, in reference to the Navy, and all other kind of Military preparations for Defence (and offence upon juſt Occaſion given) will render us Wiſe and Hounourable in eſteem of other Nations, and conſequently oblige them not only to admit us the Freedom of Trade with them, but the better terms for, and countenance in, the courſe of our Trade.

2. To make it the Intereſt of others to Trade with us, we muſt be ſure to furniſh them at as cheap or cheaper Rates than any other Nation can or doth; and this I affirm can never be done without ſubduing *Uſury* eſpecially, and doing thoſe other things before mentioned, that will conduce to the encreaſe of our Hands and Stock; for our being in a condition to ſell our Neighbours cheaper than others, muſt be when it is principally an effect of many hands and much Stock.

Objection; But it may be ſaid, How ſhall we profit by this Rule of ſelling cheap to Foreigners, whereas the contrary is ſaid to be the way to Riches, *viz.* to ſell dear, and buy cheap?

Anſw. I anſwer, in a ſtrict ſence it may be ſo for the private *Merchant*; but in this diſcourſe I am deſigning how our publick National Trade may be ſo managed, that other

Nations

Nations, who are in Competition with us for the ſame, may not wreſt it from us, but that ours may continue and encreaſe, to the diminution of theirs; if there were no others to wage with us, we might, as the Proverb ſaith, make our own Markets; but as the caſe now ſtands, that all the World are ſtriving to engroſs all the Trade they can, that other Proverb is very true and applicable, *All Covet, all Loſe.*

3. The well contrivement and management of foreign Treaties, may very much contribute to the making it the Intereſt of other Nations to Trade with us, at leaſt to the convincing of Foreign *Princes* wherein and how it is their Intereſt to Trade with us.

4. *Publick Juſtice and Honeſty* will make it the Intereſt of other Nations to Trade with us, that is, that when any Commodities paſs under a publick common Seal (which is in a kind the puklick Faith of the Nation) they may be exact in length, breadth and nature, according to what they ought to be by their Seals.

The like care ought to be taken for the true packing of our *Herrings* and *Pilchards*, (formerly mentioned.)

5 If we would engage other Nations to Trade with us, we muſt receive from them the

the Fruits and Commodities of their Countries, as well as ſend them ours; but *it's our Intereſt by Example and other means* (not diſtaſtful) *above all kinds of Commodities to prevent, as much as may be, the Importation of Foreign* Manufactures.

6. The *Venetians* being a People that take from us very little of our Manufactures, have prohibited our *Engliſh Cloath*, and from whoſe Territories we receive great quantities of Currans, purchaſed with our ready Money; it ſeems to me advantagious for *England*, that, that Importation, as well as the Importation of wrought-Glaſs, drinking-Glaſſes and other Manufactures from thence, ſhould be diſcouraged; it being ſuppoſed we can now make them as well our ſelves in *England*.

The Trade for *Canary* Wines, I take to be a moſt pernicious Trade to *England*, becauſe thoſe *Iſlands* conſume very little of our *Manufactures*, *Fiſh*, or other *Engliſh Commodities*; neither do they furniſh us with any Commodities to be further Manufactured here or re-Exported; the Wines we bring from thence being for the moſt part purchaſed with ready Money; ſo that, to my apprehenſion, ſomething is neceſſary to be done to compel thoſe *Iſlanders* to ſpend more of our *Engliſh Commodities*, and to ſell their Wines cheaper (which every Year they advance

vance in Price) or else to lessen the consumption of them in *England*.

I have in this last Discourse of the **Ballance of Trade**, as well as in my former, confined my self to write only general Heads and Principles that relate unto Trade in general, not this or that particular Trade; because the several Trades to several Countries, may require distinct and particular considerations, respecting the time, place, competitors with us, and other circumstances, to find out, wherein our advantages or disadvantages lye, and how to improve the former, and prevent the latter; but as this would be too great a Work for one Man, so fear it would make this too great a Book o be well read and considered.

But in the *Preface* to this Treatise, I have briefly mentioned many particular Trades hat we have lost, and are losing, and by what means; and many Trades that we yet etain and are encreasing, and how it happens to be so; which may give some light to clearer Discovery and Inspection into particular Trades, unto which Ingenious Men hat have Hearts to serve their *Country* in his (so necessary Work at this time) may dd, and further improve, by the advantage f Abilities to express their Sentiments in a nore Intelligible and Plausible Stile; but

 when

when I and others have said all we can, *A low Interest is, as the Soul to the Body of Trade, it is the* **Sine qua non** *to the Prosperity and Advancement of the Lands and Trades of* England.

CHAP. X.

Concerning Plantations

THE *Trade* of our *English* Plantations in *America*, being now of as great Bulk, and Employing as much Shipping as most of the Trades of this Kingdom, it seems not unnecessary to Discourse more at large concerning the Nature of *Plantations*, and the good or evil Consequences of them, in Relation to this and other Kingdoms; and the rather because some *Gentlemen* of no mean Capacities, are of Opinion, that his *Majesty's Plantations* abroad have very much Prejudiced this *Kingdom*, by draining us of our People; for the Confirmation of which Opinion they urge the Example of *Spain*, which, they say, is almost ruined by the Depopulation which the *West-Indies* hath occasioned, to the end therefore a more particular Scrutiny may be made into this matter,

I shall humbly offer my Opinion in the following Propositions, and then give those Reasons of Probability which presently occur to my Memory, in confirmation of each Proposition.

1. First, I agree, *That Lands* (though excellent) *without Hands proportionable will not enrich any Kingdom.*

2. *That whatever tends to the Depopulating of a Kingdom, tends to the Impoverishment of it.*

3. *That most Nations in the Civilized Parts of the World, are more or less Rich or Poor proportionably to the Paucity or Plenty of their People, and not to the Sterility or Fruitfulness of their Lands.*

4. *I do not agree that our People in* England *are in any considerable measure abated by reason of our Foreign Plantations; but propose to prove the contrary.*

5. *I am of Opinion, that we had immediately before the late Plague, many more People in* England, *than we had before the Inhabiting of* Virginia, New England, Barbadoes, *and the rest of our* American *Plantations.*

6. *That all Colonies or Plantations do endamage their Mother-Kingdoms, whereof the Trades of such Plantations are not confined by severe Laws, and good Executions of those Laws, to the Mother-Kingdom.*

7. *That the* Dutch *will reap the greatest ad-*

vantage by all Colonies issuing from any Kingdom of Europe, *whereof the Trades are not so strictly confined to the proper Mother-Kingdoms.*

8. *That the* Dutch (tho' they thrive so exceedingly in Trade) *will in probability never endamage this Kingdom by the growth of their Plantations.*

9. *That neither the* French, Spaniard, *nor* Portugeez *are much to be feared on that account;* not for the same, *but for other causes.*

10. *That it is more for the advantage of* England, *that* New-found-Land *should remain unplanted, than that Colonies should be sent or permitted to go thither to Inhabit, with a Governour, Laws,* &c.

11. *That* New-England *is the most prejudicial Plantation to the Kingdom of* England.

I. *That Lands, tho' in their Nature excellently good, without Hands proportionable, will not enrich any Kingdom.*

This first *Proposition* I suppose will readily be assented to by all judicious Persons, and therefore, for the proof of it, I shall only alledge a matter of Fact.

The Land of Palestine, *once the Richest Country in the Universe, since it came under the* Turks *Dominion, and consequently unpeopled, is now become the Poorest.*

Andaluzia and *Granada*, formerly wonderful Rich, and full of good Towns, since dis-

dis-peopled by the *Spaniard* by expulsion of the *Moors*, many of their Towns and brave Country-Houses are fallen into Rubbish, and their whole Country into miserable Poverty, though their Lands naturally are prodigiously Fertil.

A Hundred other Instances of Fact might be given to the like purpose.

II. *What-ever tends to the populating of a Kingdom, tends to the emprovement of it.*

The former *Proposition* being granted, I suppose this will not be denied, and of the means (*viz.* Good Laws) whereby any Kingdom may be Populated, and consequently Enriched, is, in effect, the substance and design of all my foregoing Discourse, to which, for avoiding Repetition, I must pray the Reader's Retrospection.

III. *That most Nations in the civilized parts of the World, are more or less Rich or Poor, proportionable to the paucity or plenty of their People.*

This third is a consequent of the two former Propositions: And the whole *World* is a witness to the Truth of it: *The seven united Provinces are certainly the most Populous Tract of Land in* Christendom, *and, for their bigness, undoubtedly the richest. England*, for its bigness, except our *Forrests*, *Wastes* and *Commons*, which by our own Laws and Customs are barred from Improvement, I hope, is yet a more Populous Country than *France*, and consequently Richer; I say, in proportion to its bigness: *Italy* in like proportion more Populous than *France*, and Richer; and *France* more Populous and Richer than *Spain*, &c.

IV. *I do not agree that our People in* England *are in any considerable measure abated, by reason of our Foreign Planeations, but purpose to prove the contrary.*

This I know is a controverted Point, and do believe that where there is one Man of my mind, there may be a thousand of the contrary; but I hope when the follwing grounds of my *Opinion* have been throughly examined, there will not be so many Dissenters.

That very many People now go, and have gone from this *Kingdom*, almost every Year for these sixty Years past, aud have and do settle in our Foreign Plantations, is most certain. But the first Question will be, *Whether if* England *had no Foreign Plantations for those People to be Transported unto, they could or would have stayed and lived at home with us?*

I am of opinion they never would nor could.

To resolve this Question, we must consider what kind of People they were, and are, that have and do Transport themselves to our Foreign Plantations.

New-

New-England (*as every one knows*) *was originally Inhabited, and hath since successively been Replenish'd, by a sort of People called* Puritans, which could not conform to the *Ecclesiastical Laws of* England; but being wearied with *Church Censures and Persecutions*, were forced to quit their Fathers Land, to find out new Habitations, as many of them did in *Germany* and *Holland*, as well as at *New-England*; and had there not been a *New-England* found for some of them, *Germany* and *Holland* probably had received the rest: But *Old England to be sure had lost them all.*

Virginia *and* Barbadoes *were first peopled by a sort of loose vagrante Pople*, vicious and destitute of means to live at home (being either unfit for Labour, or such as could find none to employ themselves about, or had so mis-behaved themselves by *Whoreing, Thieving*, or other *Debauchery*, that none would set them on work) which *Merchants* and *Masters* of Ships by their Agents (*or* Spirits, *as they were called*) gathered up about the Streets of *London*, and other places, cloathed and transported to be employed upon Plantations; and these, I say, were such as, had there been no *English* Foreign Plantation in the World, could probably never have lived at home to do service for their Country, but must have come to be hanged, or starved, or dyed untimely of ſome of thoſe miſerable Diſeaſes, that proceed from want and vice; or elſe have ſold themſelves for Soldiers, to be knock'd on the Head, or ſtarved, in the Quarrels of our Neighbours, as many thouſands of brave *Engliſh-men* were, in the low-Countries, as alſo in the Wars of *Germany*, *France* and *Sweeden*, &c. or elſe, if they could, by begging, or otherwiſe, arrive to the Stock of 2 *s.* 6 *d.* to waft them over to *Holland*, become Servants to the *Dutch*, who refuſe none.

But the *principal Growth* and *Encreaſe* of the aforeſaid *Plantations* of *Virginia* and *Barbadoes* happened in, or immediately after, our late Civil Wars, when the worſted party by the fate of War, being deprived of their *Eſtates*, and having ſome of them never been bred to labour, and others made unfit for it by the lazy habit of a Soldiers Life, there wanting Means to maintain them all abroad with his *Majeſty*, many of them betook themſelves to the aforeſaid *Plantations*, and great numbers of *Scotch Soldiers* of his *Majeſty*'s Army, after *Woreſter Fight*, were by the then prevailing Powers voluntarily ſent thither.

Another great *ſwarm*, or acceſſion of new Inhabitants to the aforeſaid *Plantations*, as alſo to *New England*, *Jamaica*, and all other his

Majeſties

Majesties Plantations in the *West-Indies*, ensued upon his *Majesties* Restouration, when the former prevailing party being by a Divine Hand of Providence brought under, the *Army* disbanded, many *Officers* displaced, and all the new *purchasers* of publick Titles dispossest of their pretended Lands, Estates, *&c.* many became impoverished, destitute of employment; and therefore such as could find no way of living at home, *and some which feared the re-establishment of the Ecclesiastical Laws, under which they could not live*, were forced to transport themselves, or sell themselves for a few Years, to be transported by others to the Foreign *English* Plantations: The constant supply that the said Plantations have since had, hath been such vagrant loose People, as I have before-mentioned, picked up, especially about the Streets and Suburbs of *London* and *Westminster*, and Malefactors Condemned for Crimes, for which by the Law they deserved to dye; *and some of those People called* Quakers, *Banished for meeting on pretence of Religious Worship.*

Now, if from the Premises it be duly considered what kind of Persons those have been, by which our Plantations have at all times been replenished, I suppose it will appear that such they have been, and under

such

ſuch Circumſtances, that if his *Majeſty* had had no Foreign Plantations, to which they might have reſorted, *England* however muſt have loſt them.

To illuſtrate the truth whereof a little further, let us conſider what Captain *Graunt*, the Ingenious *Author of the Obſervations upon the Bills of Mortality*, ſaith, Page 76. and in other places of his Book, concerning the City of *London*; and it is not only ſaid, but undeniably proved, *viz. That the City of* London, *let the Mortality be what it will, by Plague, or otherwiſe, repairs its Inhabitants once in two Years.* And Page 101. again, *If there be encouragement for a Hundred Perſons in* London (that is, a way how a Hundred may live better than in the Country) *the evacuating of a fourth or third part of that number muſt ſoon be ſupplied out of the Country, who in a ſhort time remove themſelves from thence hither, ſo long until the City, for want of receipt and encouragement, regurgitates and ſends them back.*

1. What he hath proved concerning *London*, I ſay of *England* in general; and the ſame may be ſaid of any Kingdom or Country in the World.

Such as our employment is for People, ſo many will our People be; and if we ſhould imagin we have in *England* employment but for one

one hundred People, and we have born and bred amongst us one hundred and fifty People; I say, the fifty must away from us, or starve, or be hanged to prevent it, whether we had any Foreign *Plantations* or not.

2. If by reason of the accommodation of living in our Foreign *Plantations*, we have evacuated more of our People than we should have done, if we had no such *Plantations*, I say, with the aforesaid *Author* in the case of *London*; and if that evacuation be grown to an excess (which I believe it never did barely on the account of the Plantations) that decrease would procure its own Remedy; for much want of People would procure greater Wages, and greater Wages, if our *Laws* gave encouragement, would procure us a supply of People without the charge of breeding them, as the *Dutch* are, and always have been, supplied in their greatest Extremities.

Object. But it may be said, Is not the Facility of being Transported into the Plantations, together with the enticing Methods Customarily used to perswade People to go thither, and the encouragement of living there with a People that speak our own *Language*, strong Motives to draw our People from us; and do they not draw more from us, than otherwise would leave us, to go into Foreign Countries, where they understand not the *Language*?

I

I anſwer; 1*ſt*, It is not much more difficult to get a paſſage to *Holland*, than it is to our Plantations.

2*dly*, Many of thoſe that go to our Plantations, if they could not go thither, would and muſt go into Foreign Countries, tho' it were ten times more difficult to get thither than it is; or elſe, which is worſe (as hath been ſaid) would adventure to be hanged, to prevent begging or ſtarving, as too many have done.

3*dly*, I do acknowledge that the facility of getting to the *Plantations*, may cauſe ſome more to leave us, than would do if they had none but Foreign Countries for Refuge: But then if it be conſidered, that our *Plantations* ſpending moſtly our *Engliſh* Manufactures, and thoſe of all ſorts almoſt imaginable, in egregious quantities, and employing near two thirds of all our *Engliſh Shipping, do therein give a conſtant Suſtenance to, may be, two hundred thouſand Perſons here at home*; then I muſt needs conclude upon the whole matter, *That we have not the fewer, but the more People in* England, *by reaſon of our* Engliſh *Plantations in* America.

Object. 2. But it may be ſaid, Is not this inferring and arguing againſt Senſe and Experience? Doth not all the World ſee that the many Noble *Kingdoms* of *Spain* in *Europe*,

are

are almost depopoulated and ruinated, by reason of their Peoples flocking over to the *West-Indies*? And do not all other Nations diminish in People after they become possessed of Foreign Plantations?

Answ. 1. I answer, With submission to better Judgments, that in my Opinion, *Contending for uniformity in Religion hath contributed ten times more to the depopulating of* Spain, *than all the* American *Plantations:* What was it but that which caused the expulsion of so many thousand *Moores*, who had Built and Inhabited most of the chief *Cities* and *Towns* of *Andaluzia*, *Granada*, *Aragon*, and other parts? What was it but that, and the *Inquisition*, that hath and doth daily expel such vast numbers of Rich *Jews* with their Families and Estates, into *Germany*, *Italy*, *Turkey*, *Holland* and *England*? What was it but that which caused those vast and long Wars between that *King* and the *low Countries*, and the effusion of so much *Spanish Blood*, and Treasure, and the final loss of the *Seven Provinces*, which we now see so Prodigious Rich, and full of People, while *Spain* is empty and poor, and *Flanders* thin and weak, in continual fear of being made a prey to their Neighbours?

2. I answer, We must warily distinguish between Country and Country; for though

Plan-

Plantations may have drained *Spain* of People, it does not follow that they have or will drain *England* or *Holland*, because where Liberty and Property are not so well preserved, and where Interest of Money is permitted to go at 12 *per cent*, there can be no considerable Manufacturing, and no more of Tillage and Grazing, than, as we Proverbially say, will keep Life and Soul together; and where there is little Manufacturing, and as little Husbandry of Lands, the profit of *Plantations*, viz. the greatest part thereof, will not redound to the Mother-Kingdom, but to other Countries, wherein there are more Manufactures and more Productions from the Earth; from hence it follows, *Plantations* thus managed prove drains of the Plople from their Mother-Kingdom; whereas Plantations belonging to Mother-Kingdoms or Countries, where Liberty and Property is better preserved, and Interest of Money restrained to a low Rate, the consequence is, that every Person sent abroad with the *Negroes* and *Utensils*, he is constrained to employ, or that are employed with him; it being Customary in most of our *Islands* in *America*, upon every Plantation, to employ eight or ten Blacks for one White Servant; I say, in this case we may reckon, that for Provisions, Cloaths and

Hous-

Houshold-goods, Sea-men, and all others employed about Materials for Building, Fitting and Victualling of Ships, *Every* English-man *in* Barbadoes *or* Jamaica *creates employment for four men at home.*

3*dly*, I answer, That *Holland* now sends as many, and more, People Yearly to reside in their *Plantations*, *Fortresses* and *Ships* in the *East-Indies* (besides many into the *West-Indies*) than *Spain*, and yet is so far from declining in the Number of their People at home that it is evident they do monstruously encrease: And so I hope, under the next Head, to prove that *England* hath constantly encreased in People at home, since our settlement upon *Plantations* in *America*, altho' not in so great a Proportion as the *Dutch.*

V. *I am of Opinion, that we had, immediately before the late Plague, more People in* England, *than we had before the Inhabiting of* New-England, Virginia, Barbadoes, *&c.*

The proof of this at best I know can but be conjectural; but in Confirmation of my *Opinion*, I have, I think, of my mind the most Industrious *English Calculator* this Age hath produced in publick, *viz.* Captain *Graunt* in the forementioned Treatise, Page 88. his words are, '*Upon the whole matter we* '*may therefore conclude, that the People of the* '*whole Nation do encrease, and consequently the* '*decrease*

'*decrease of* Winchester, Lincoln, *and other* '*like places, must be attributed to other Reasons than that of refurnishing* London *only.*

2. It is manifest by the aforesaid worthy *Author*'s Calculations, that the Inhabitants of *London*, and parts adjacent, have encreased to almost double within this sixty Years; and that City hath usually been taken for an Index of the whole.

I know it will be said, that altho' *London* have so encreased, othur parts have so much diminished, whererеof some are named before; but if to answer the diminution of Inhabitants in some particular places, it be considered how others are encreased, *viz.* *Yarmouth*, *Hull*, *Scarebrough*, and other Ports in the *North*, as also *Leverpool*, *Westchester* and *Bristol*; *Portsmouth*, *Lime* and *Plimouth*; and withal, if it be considered what great Improvements have been made this last sixty Years upon breaking up and enclosing of Wastes, Forrests and Parks, and draining of the *Fens*, and all those places Inhabited and Furnished with Husbandry, *&c.* then I think it will appear probable that we have in *England* now, at least had before the late *Plague*, more People than we had before we first entered upon Foreign *Plantations*, notwithstanding likewise the great Numbers of Men which have issued from us into *Ireland*;

which

which Country, as our Laws now are, I reckon not among the number of Plantations profitable to *England*, nor within the limits of this Diſcourſe, altho' peradventure ſomething may be pickt out of theſe Papers, which may deſerve conſideration in relation to that Country.

But it may be ſaid, If we have more People now than in former Ages, how came it to paſs that, in the times of King *Henry the fourth and fifth*, and other times formerly, we could raiſe ſuch great Armies, and employ them in foreign Wars, and yet retain a ſufficient number to defend the *Kingdom*, and cultivate our Lands at home?

I anſwer; *Firſt*, the bigneſs of Armies is not always a certain Indication of the numerouſneſs of a Nation, but ſometimes rather of the nature of the Government, and Diſtribution of the Lands; as for Inſtance, Where the *Prince and Lords* are owners of the whole Territory, altho' the People be thin, the Armies upon occaſion may be very great, as in *Eaſt-India*, *Turky*, and the Kingdoms of *Feſſe* and *Morocco*, where *Tafelet* was lately ſaid to have an *Army* of one hundred and fifty, or two hundred, thouſand Men, altho' every body knows that Country hath as great a ſcarcity of People as any in the World: But ſince *Free-holders* are ſo much encreased in *England*, and the servile *Tenures* altered, doubtless it is more difficult, as well as more chargeable, to draw great *numbers* of Men into foreign Wars.

2. Since the Introduction of the new *Artillery of Powder*, Shot and Fire-Arms into the World, all War is become as much rather an expence of Money as Men, and success attends those that can most and longest spend Money, rather than Men; and consequently *Princes Armies in* Europe *are become more proportionable to their Purses than to the Numbers of their People.*

VI. *That all Colonies and foreign Plantations do endamage their Mother-Kingdoms, whereof the Trades (of such Plantations) are not confined to their said Mother-Kingdoms, by good Laws and severe Execution of those Laws.*

1. *The practice of all the Governments of* Europ witness *to the Truth of this Proposition.* Th *Danes* keep the Trade of *Izland* to them selves: The *Dutch*, *Surrenham*, and all thei Settlements in *East-India:* The *French*, St *Christophers*, and their other Plantations i the *West-Indies:* The *Portugeeze*, *Brazil*, an all the Coasts thereof: The *Spaniards*, a their vast Territories upon the Main in th *West-Indies*, and many Islands there; and o own Laws seem to design the like, as to a our Plantations in *New-England*, *Virgini*

Ba

Barbadoes,&c. altho' we have not yet arrived to a compleat and effectual Execution of those Laws.

2. *Plantations* being at first furnished, and afterwards successively supplied with People from their Mother-Kingdoms, and People being Riches, that loss of People to the Mother-Kingdoms,be it more or less, is certainly a damage, except the employment of those People abroad, do cause the employment of so many more at home in their Mother-Kingdoms; and that can never be, except the Trade be restrained to their Mother-Kingdom, which will not be doubted by any that understands the next Proposition, *&c.*

VII. *That the* Dutch *will reap the greatest advantage by all Colonies,issuing from any Kingdom in* Europe, *whereof the Trades are not so strictly confined to their proper Mother-kingdoms.*

This *Proposition* will readily be assented unto by any that understand the nature of *low Interest* and *low Customs*; where the Market is free, they shall be sure to have the Trade that can sell the best penny-worths, that buy dearest and sell cheapest,which(Nationally speaking) none can do but those that have Money at the lowest rate of *Interest*,and pay the least *Customs*, which are the *Dutch*; and this is the true cause why, before the

Act of Navigation, there went ten *Dutch* Ships to *Barbadoes* for one *English*.

VIII. *That the Dutch* (tho' they thrive so exceedingly in Trade) *will in probability never endamage this Kingdom by the growth of their Plantations.*

1. In fact, the *Dutch* never did much thrive in planting, for I do remember, they had, about twenty Years past, *Tabago*, a most fruitful *Island* in the *West-Indies*, apt for the production of *Sugars* and all other Commodities that are propagated in *Barbadoes*, and, as I have heard Planters affirm, better accommodated with Rivers for Water-Mills, which are of great use for grinding of the Canes; this *Island* is still in their possession, and *Corasoa*, and some others, and about sixteen or seventeen Years past they were so eager upon the Improvement of it, that, besides what they did in *Holland*, they set up Bills upon the *Exchange* in *London*, proffering great Priviledges to any that would Transport themselves thither. Notwithstanding all which, to this day, that *Island* is not the tenth part so well improved as *Jamaica* hath been by the *English* within these five Years; neither have the *Dutch* at any other time, or in any other parts of the World, made any Improvement by Planting; what they do in the *East-Indies* being

only

only by War, Trade and Building of Fortified Towns and Castles, upon the Sea-Coasts, to secure the sole Commerce of the Places; and with the People which they Conquer not, by clearing, breaking up of the Ground, and Planting as the *English* have done.

This I take to be a strong Argument of Fact to my present purpose.

2. The second Argument to prove this Proposition is from Reason: I have before mentioned the several Accidents and Methods by which our Foreign Plantations have from time to time come to be Peopled and emproved.

Now the *Dutch* being void of those Accidents, are destitute of the occasions to emprove foreign Plantations by digging and delving as the *English* have done.

For 1*st*. In *Holland* their *Interest* and *Customs* being low, together with their other Encouragements to Trade, mentioned in the former parts of this Treatise, gives Employment to all their People born and bred amongst them, and also to multitudes of Foreigners.

2. *Their giving Liberty, or at least Connivance to all Religions, as well* Jews *and* Roman-Catholicks, *as* Sectaries, gives security to all their Inhabitants at home, and expels

none, nor puts a necessity upon any to Banish themselves upon that account.

3. Their careful and wonderful Providing for and employing their *Poor* at home, puts all their People utterly out of Danger of Starving, or necessity of Stealing, and consequently out of fear of Hanging. I might add to this, that they have not for a long time had any Civil-War among them; and from the whole conclude, that the *Dutch* as they did never, so they never can or will thrive by Planting; and that our *English* Plantations abroad are a good effect, proceeding from many evil causes.

IX. *That neither the* French, Spaniards *or* Portugeeze *are much to be feared on the account of Planting; not for the same, but for other Reasons.*

That the *French* have had footing in the *West-Indies*, almost as long as the *English*, is certain, and that they have made no considerable progress in Planting is as certain; and finding it so in Fact, I have been often exercising my thoughts about enquiry into the reason thereof, which I attribute especially to two.

First, Because *France* being an absolute Government, hath not, until very lately given any Countenance or Encouragement to *Navigation* and *Trade*.

Second-

Secondly and principally, because the *French* Settlements in the *West-Indies* have not been upon *Freeholders* as the *English* are, but in subjection to the *French West-India Company*, which *Company* being under the *French King*, as *Lord Proprietor* of the places they settle upon, and taxing the *Inhabitants* at pleasure as the King doth them, it is not probable they should make that successful Progress in Planting; *Propriety, Freedom and Inheritance being the most effectual Spurs to Industry*.

2. Tho' some (who have not looked far into this Matter) may think the *Spaniards* have made great Progress in Planting, I am of opinion, that the *English*, since the time they set upon this Work, have cleared and improved fifty Plantations for one, and Built as many Houses for one the *Spaniards* have Built; this will not be very difficult to imagine, if it be considered.

First, that it is not above fifty or sixty Years since the *English* intended the propagating Foreign Plantations.

Secondly, that the *Spaniards* were possessed of the *West-Indies* about our *King Henry* the 7*th*'s time, which is near two Hundred Years past.

Thirdly, that what the *Spaniard* hath done in the *West-Indies* hath been ten times more by Conquest than Planting.

Fourthly, That the *Spaniards* found in the *West-Indies* most of the Cities and Towns ready Built and Inhabited, and much of the Ground improved and cultivated before their coming thither.

Fifthly, That the *Inhabitants* which they found there, and subdued, were such a People with whom some of the *Spaniards* could and have mixed, from whence hath proceeded a Generation of People which they call *Mistises*; whereas the *English* where they have set down and Planted, either found none, or such as were meer wild *Heathen*, with whom they could not, nor ever have been known to mix.

Sixthly, That now after such a long series of time, the *Spaniards* are scarce so populous in any part of the *West-Indies*, as to be able to bring an Army of *Ten Thousand* Men together in a Months time.

From all which I conjecture.

1st. *That his Majesty hath now more* English Subjects *in all his Foreign Plantations, in sixty Years, than the King of* Spain *hath* Spaniards *in all his, in two hundred Years.*

2d. *That the* Spaniards *progress in Planting bears no proportion to the encrease of the* English *Plantations.*

3d. That seeing the *Spaniards*, in the time of their greatest prosperity, and under so

many

many Advantages, have been such indifferent Planters, and have made such slow progress in Peopling those parts of the *West-Indies*, which they possess, *It is not much to be feared that ever the* English *will be mated by the* Spaniards *in their Foreign Plantations, or production of the Native Commodities of those parts.*

Now the reasons why the *Spaniards* are so thin of People in the *West-Indies*, I take to be such as these following, *viz.*

First and Principally, *because they exercise the same Policy and Governments, Civil and Ecclesiastical, in their Plantations, as they do in their Mother-Kingdom*; from whence it follows that their People are few and thin abroad, from the same causes as they are empty and void of People at home; whereas altho' *we in* England *vainly endeavour to arrive at a Uniformity of Religion at home, yet we allow an* Amsterdam *Liberty in our Plantations.*

It is true, *New-England* being a more Independant Government from this Kingdom than any other of our Plantations, and the People that went thither more one peculiar Sort or Sect, than those that went to the rest of our Plantations, they did, for some Years past, exercise some severities against the *Quakers*; but of late they have understood their true Interest better, insomuch as I have not heard of any Act of that kind for these

five

five or six Years last, notwithstanding am well informed, that there are now amongst them many more *Quakers* and other *Dissenters* from their Forms of Religious Worship, than were at the time of their greatest Severity, which severity had no other effect but to encrease the *New-English Non-Conformists*.

2*d*. A second reason why the Productions of the *Spanish-West-India* Commodities are so inconsiderable in respect to the *English*, and consequently why their progress in Planting hath been, and is like to be, much less than the *English*, as also the encrease of their People, I take to be the dearness of the Freight of their Ships, which is four times more than our *English* Freight; and if you would know how that comes to be so, twelve *per cent* Interest will go a great way towards the satisfying you, altho' there are other concomitant lesser causes, which whosoever understands *Spain*, or shall carefully read this Treatise, may find out themselves.

3*d*. A third reason I take to be the greatness of the *Customs* in *Old-Spain*, for undoubtedly *high Customs do as well dwarf Plantations as Trade*.

4. The *Spaniards* Intense and singular Industry in their Mines for Gold and Silver, the

the working wherein destroys abundance of their People, at least of their Slaves, doth cause them to neglect in great measure Cultivating of the Earth, and producing Commodities from the growth thereof, which might give employment to a greater Navy, as well as sustenance to a far greater number of People by Sea and Land.

5*th*. Their multitude of *Fryers, Nuns and other reclup'd and Ecclesiastical Persons*, which are prohibited from *Marriage*.

3. The third sort of People I am to Discourse of, are the *Portugeeze*, and them I must acknowledge to have been great Planters in the *Brazeils* and other places; but yet if we preserve our People and Plantations by good Laws, I have reason to believe, that the *Portugeeze* (except they alter their Politicks, which is almost impossible for them to do) can never bear up with us, much less prejudice our Plantations.

That hitherto they have not hurt us, but we them, is most apparent; for in my time we have beat their *Muscovado* and *Paneal Sugars* quite out of use in *England*, and their *Whites* we have brought down in all these Parts of *Europe* in price, from seven and eight Pounds *per Cent*, to fifty Shillings and three Pounds *per Cent*, and in quantity; whereas formerly their *Brazeil-Fleets* consisted of one

Hun-

Hundred, to one Hundred and twenty thousand *Chests of Sugar*, they are now reduced to about thirty Thousand *Chests*, since the great encrease of *Barbadoes*.

The reason of this decay of the Portugeeze *productions in Brazeils is certainly the better policy than our* English *Plantations are founded upon.*

That which principally dwarfs the *Portugeeze Plantations* is the same before mentioned which hinders the *Spaniards*, viz. *extraordinary high Customs at home, high Freights, high Interest of Mony, Ecclesiastical Persons*, &c.

From all that hath been said concerning Plantations in general, I draw these two Principal Conclusions.

1*st*. *That our* English Plantations *may thrive beyond any other* Plantations *in the World, tho' the Trades of all of them were more severely limited by Laws and good Execution of these Laws to their Mother Kingdom of* England, *exclusive to* Ireland *and* New-England.

2dly, *That it is in his* Majesties *Power, and the* Parliaments, *if they please, by taking off all Charges from Sugar, to make it more intirely an* English Commodity, *than white-Herrings are a* Dutch Commodity, *and to draw more profit to this Kingdom thereby, than the* Dutch *do by that: And that in consequence thereof, all Plantations*

tations

tations of other Nations must in few Years sink to little or nothing.

X. *That it is more for the Advantage of* England *that* New-fonnd-land *should remain unplanted, than that Colonies should be sent or permitted to go thither to Inhabit under a Governour, Laws,* &c.

I have before discoursed of *Plantations* in general, most of the *English* being in their Nature much a like, except this of *New-found-land*, and that of *New-England*, which I intend next to speak of.

The advantage *New-found-land* hath brought to this Kingdom is only by the Fishery there, and of what vast concernment that is, is well known to most *Gentlemen and Merchants*, especially those of the *West* parts of *England*, from whence especially this Trade is driven.

It is well known, upon undeniable proof, that in the Year, 1605. The *English* employed 250 Sail of Ships small and great, in Fishing upon that Coast; and it is now too apparent, that we do not so employ from all Parts, above eighty Sail of Ships.

It is likewise generally known and confessed, that when we employed so many Ships in that Trade, the current price of our Fish in that Country, was (*Communibus annis*) seventeen Rials, which is eight Shillings six

Pence

Pence *per* Quintail, and that ſince, as we have leſſened in that Trade, the *French* have encreaſed in it, and that we have annually proceeded to raiſe our Fiſh from ſeventeen Rials to twenty four Rials, or twelve Shillings, (*Communibus annis*) as it now ſells in the Country.

This being the Caſe of *England* in relation to this Trade, it is certainly worth the enquiry.

1ſt, *How we came to decay in that Trade.*

2dly, *What means may be uſed to recover our ancient Greatneſs in that Trade, or at leaſt to prevent our further diminution therein?*

The decay of that Trade I attribute,

Firſt, and Principally, to the growing Liberty which is every Year more and more uſed in *Romiſh Countries*, as well as others, of eating Fleſh in *Lent* and on Fiſh-days.

2. To a late abuſe crept into that Trade, (which hath much abated the expence within theſe twenty Years of that Commodity) of ſending over private *Boat-keepers*, which hath much diminiſhed the number of the *Fiſhing-Ships*.

3. To the great encreaſe of the *French Fiſhery of Placentia* and other Ports on the back ſide of *New-found-land*.

4. To the ſeveral *Wars* we have had at Sea within theſe twenty Years, which have much

much empoveriſhed the *Merchants* of our *Weſtern* Parts, and reduced them to carry on a great part of that Trade at *Bottumry*, *viz.* Money taken upon adventure of the Ship at twenty *per cent per Annum.*

2. *What means may be uſed to recover our ancient greatneſs in that Trade, or at leaſt to prevent our farther diminution therein.*

For this, two contrary ways have been propounded.

1. To ſend a *Governour* to reſide there, and to encourage People to Inhabit there, as well for defence of the Country againſt Invaſion, as to manage the *Fiſhery* there by Inhabitants upon the place; this hath often been propounded by the *Planters* and ſome *Merchants* of *London*.

2. The ſecond way propounded, and which is directly contrary to the former, is by the *Weſt-Country Merchants* and Owners of the *Fiſhing-Ships*, and that is, to have no *Governour* nor *Inhabitants* permitted to reſide at *New-found-land*, nor any *Paſſengers*, or private *Boat-keepers* ſuffered to Fiſh at *New-found-land.*

This latter way propounded is moſt agreeable to my propoſition, and, if it could be effected, I am perſwaded would revive the decayed *Engliſh-Fiſhing-Trade* at *New-found-land*, and be otherwiſe greatly for the

ad-

advantage of this *Kingdom*; and that for these following Reasons.

1. Because *most of the Provisions the* Planters *which are settled at* New-found-land *do make use of, viz.* Bread, Beef, Pork, Butter, Cheese, Cloaths, and *Irish*-Bandal, Cloth, Linnen and Woolen, *Irish*-Stockings, *as also* Nets, Hooks *and* Lines, *&c. they are supplied with from* New-England *and* Ireland; *and with* Wine, Oyl *and* Linnen *by the Salt Ships from* France *and* Spain, *in consequence whereof the Labour, as well as the feeding and Clothing of so many Men, is lost to* England.

2. The *Planters* settled there, being mostly loose vagrant People, and without Order and Government, do keep dissolute Houses, which have Debauch'd Sea-men, and diverted them from their Laborious and Industrious Calling; whereas before there were settlements there, the Sea-men had no other resort during the Fishing Season (being the time of their abode in that Country) but to their Ships, which afforded them convenient Food and Repose, without the inconveniencies of Excess.

3. If it be the Interest of all Trading Nations principally to encourage Navigation, and to promote especially those Trades which employ most Shipping: Than which nothing is more true, and more regarded by

h, then certainly it is the Inte-
nd to diſcountenance and abate
of Planters at *New-found-land*;
uld e[illegible]aſe, it would in a few
to [illegible]ng in relation to that
it hath to the *Fiſhery* at *New-*
ch many years ſince was mana-
Ships from the Weſtern Ports;
ations there encreaſed, fell to
mployment of People ſettled
othing of that Trade left the
ſh-men, but the liberty of car-
l then, by courteſie or purchaſe,
g of Fiſh to *Bilvoa*, when their
liſh Shiping are better Employ-
leiſure to do it.

ifeſt that before there were Boat-
nters at New-found-land *Fiſh*
than now it is, by about 40 *per*
quently more vended, the rea-
take to be this; the *Boat-*
nters, being generally at firſt
, and being upon that place,
fford their Fiſh cheaper than
ps from *Old England*, ſo doubt-
firſt as well at *New-England*
d-land, until they had beat
ips out of the Trade; after
reed from that competition,
azy as to that laborious em-

 ployment

ployment, having means oth
and employ themſelves, and t
haunced the price of their Fi
exceſs,as in effect prove the g
that Trade to the *Fr* B who
ſaid impolitick management o
have of late Years been able to
at all Markets abroad; and m
is,that thoſe that can ſell cheap
the Trade.

5. *This Kingdom being an Iſ*
Intereſt, as well for our preſerva
fit, not only to have many Sea-me
them as much as may be within
danger. Now the Fiſhing S
in *March*, and returning hom
in the Month of *September* yea
being employed in that Trad
and fifty Ships, which migh
ten thouſand Sea-men, Fiſher-
men, as they uſually call the
ſons who were never before
peal to the Reader, whether
return of Sea-men, abiding
us all the Winter, and ſpend
ney here which they got in t
Fiſhery, were not a great ac
and Power to this Kingdom
ſupply for his *Majeſty's* Navy
gencies.

6. *The Fishing-Ships yet are, and always have been the breeders of Seamen*; the Planters and Boat-keepers are generally such as were bred, and became expert at the cost of the Owners of Fishing-Ships, which Planters and Boat-keepers enter very few new or green Men.

7. By the building, fitting, victualling and repairing of Fishing-Ships, multitudes of *English Trades-men* and *Artificers* (besides the Owners and Sea-men) gain their subsistance; whereas by the Boats which the *Planters and Boat-keepers* build or use at *New-found-land*, *England* gets nothing.

Object. But against all that I have said, those that contend for a *Governour* at *New-found land*, Object,

1. That without a *Governour* and *Government* there, that Country will be always exposed to the surprizal of the *French*, or any *Foreigners* that shall please to attack it.

2. That the disorders of the *Planters*, which I complain of (and some others, which, for brevities sake, I have not mentioned) cannot be remedied without a *Governour*.

To which I answer *first*, that when we cannot preserve our *Colonies* by our Shipping, or so awe our Neighbours by our *Fleets* and Ships of War, that they dare not attempt them, our case will be sad, and our Proprie-

ty will be lost, or in iminent
only abroad but at home likewi

2*dly*, All the *Fish* that is kil
found-land in a Summer, is not
maintain strength enough on
fend two Fishing Harbours agai
of War, whereas that Countr
Harbours to defend, than are t
Old England.

3*dly*, If a *Governour* be esta
next consequence will be a T
Fishing, and the least Tax will
price of Fish, and that unavoida
the Trade away wholly into
Hands.

4*thly*, A *Government* there i
antient Custom among the A
Fishing-Ships, to which the Fi
inured, and that free from op
adapted to the Trade, insom
tho' a better might be wished,
to see it.

XI. *That* New-England *is th*
cial Plantation to this Kingdom.

I am not to write of a People, w
Industry and Temperance, and t
whose Laws and Institution, do p
selves long Life, with a wonderf
People, Riches and Power: Aud a
ought to envy that Vertue an

ch themſelves either can or will , but rather to commend and yet I think it is the duty of every imarily to reſpect the well-fare e Country; and therefore tho' l ſome, whom I would not ſpleaſe, I cannot omit, in the this Diſcourſe, to take notice iculars, wherein *Old* England *tion by the growth of thoſe Colonies* -*England*, and how that *Planta*-om thoſe more Southerly, with e gain or loſs of this Kingdom,

American Plantations, except *England*, produce Commodities Natures from thoſe of this King-r, *Tobacco*, *Cocoa*, *Wool*, *Ginger*, f *dying Woods*, &c. Whereas l produces generally the ſame , *viz. Corn* and *Cattle*; ſome Fiſh they do likewiſe kill, but and ſaved altogether by their ants, which prejudiceth our *nd* Trade, where, as hath been ew are, or ought according to be, employed in thoſe Fiſheries itants of Old *England*.

r Commodities we have from me few *great Maſts*, *Furs*, and

Train-Oyl, whereof the Yearl
mounts to very little, the m
value of returns from thence, be
Sugar, *Cotton*, *Wool*, *Tobacco and* ſ
modities, which they firſt receiv
other of his *Majeſties Plantation*
for dry *Cod-Fiſh*, *ſalt Mackerel*,
Bread, *Beer*, *Flower*, *Peaſe*, &c.
ſupply *Barbadoes*, *Jamaica*, &c.
diminution of the vent of thoſe C
from this Kingdom; the great
whereof in our *Weſt India Planta*
ſoon be found in the advantage
of our Lands in *England*, were
the vaſt and almoſt incredible ſu
Colonies have from *New-England*.

2. The People of *New-Englan*
of their Primitive *Charters*, bei
tied to the obſervation of the L
Kingdom, do ſometimes aſſume
Trading, contrary to the *Act of*
by reaſon whereof many of o
Commodities, eſpecially *Tobacc*
are tranſported in *New-Engli*
directly into *Spain*, and other fo
tries, without being Landed in
paying any duty to his *Majeſty*,
only loſs to the *King*, and a pre
Navigation of Old England, but
excluſion of the old *Engliſh Me*

the vent of thoſe Commodities in thoſe Ports, where the *New-Engliſh* Veſſels Trade; becauſe, there being no *Cuſtom* paid on thoſe Commodities in *New-England*, and a great *Cuſtom* paid upon them in *Old-England*, it muſt neceſſarily follow that the *New-Engliſh* Merchant will be able to afford his Commodity much cheaper at the Market, than the Old *Engliſh Merchant*: And thoſe that can ſell cheapeſt, will infallibly engroſs the whole Trade ſooner or later.

3. Of all the *American Plantations*, his *Majeſty* hath none ſo apt for the building of Shipping as *New-England*, nor none comparably ſo qualified for breeding of Sea-men, not only by reaſon of the natural induſtry of that People, but principally by reaſon of their *Cod* and *Mackerel Fiſheries*: And in my poor opinion there is nothing more prejudicial, and in proſpect more dangerous to any Mother *Kingdom*, than the encreaſe of Shipping in their *Colonies*, *Plantations* or *Provinces*.

4. The People that evacuate from us to *Barbadoes*, and the other *Weſt-India Plantations*, as was before hinted, do commonly work one *Engliſh-man* to ten or eight *Blacks*; and if we keep the Trade of our ſaid *Plantations* intirely to *England*, *England* woud have no leſs Inhabitants, but rather an encreaſe

of People by such evacuation, because that one *Englishman*, with the ten *Blacks* that work with him, accounting what they eat, use and wear, would make employment for four Men in *England*, as was said before; whereas peradventure of ten Men that issue from us to *New-England* and *Ireland*, what we send to, or receive from them, doth not employ one Man in *England*.

To conclude this Chapter, and to do right to that most Industrious *English Colony*, I must confess that though we loose by their unlimited Trade with our Foreign Plantations, yet we are very great Gainers, by their direct Trade to and from Old *England*. Our Yearly Exportations of *English Manufactures*, Mault and other Goods from hence thither, amounting in my opinion to ten times the value of what is Imported from thence; which calculation I do not make at random, but upon mature consideration, and peradventure upon as much Experience in this very Trade, as any other person will pretend to; and therefore, when ever a Reformation of our Correspondency in Trade with that People shall be thought on, it will in my poor Judgment require great tenderness and very serious Circumspection.

FINIS.

A Small TREATISE Against USURY

TO leave the *Proofs* of the unlawfullneſs of Uſury to Divines, wherein a number, as well *Proteſtants* as *Papiſts*, have learnedly Written; here is only ſet down ſome Arguments to ſhew how great the hurt is, it doth to this Kingdom, which hath no Gold nor Silver *Mines*, but plenty of Commodities, and many and great advantages of Trade; to which the high rate of Uſury is a great prejudice and decay.

For Proof, how much the high rate of Uſury decays Trade; we ſee that generally all Merchants when they have gotten any great Wealth, leave Trading and fall to Uſury, the gain thereof being ſo eaſie, certain and great; whereas in other Countries, where Uſury is at a lower rate, and thereby Lands dearer to purchaſe, they continue Merchants from Generation to Generation, to enrich themſelves and the State.

Neither

Neither are they rich Trades-Men only, that give over Trading, but a number of Beginners are undone or discouraged by the high rate of Usury, their Industry serving but to enrich others, and Begger themselves.

We also see many Trades themselves much decayed, because they will not afford so great a gain as Ten in the Hundred; whereas if the rate of Usury were not higher here than in other Countries, they had still subsisted and flourished, and perhaps with as much advantage to the Publick, as those that do bring more to the Private Adventurers.

Yet are not those the greatest hinderances the high rate of Money brings to Trade; our greatest disadvantage is, that other Nations, especially our Industrious Neighbours the *Dutch*, are therein Wiser than we: For with them, and so in most Countries with whom we hold Commerce, there is not any Use for Money tollerated above the rate of Six in the Hundred: Whereby it must of necessity come to pass, though they have no other Advantages of Industry and Frugality, that they must out-Trade us; for if they make return of ten *per cent*, they almost double the Use allowed, and so make a very gainful Trade. But with us, where ten in the Hundred is so current, it is otherwise; for if we make not above ten, we are loosers and consequently the same Trade being with them and us equally good for the Publick, is to the private Adventurers lossful with us, with them very gainful. And where the good of Publick and Private Mens go not together, the Publick is seldom greatly advanced.

And as they out-Trade, so they may afford to under-sell us in the Fruits of the Earth, which are equally natural to our and their Lands, as to our great shame we see our Neighbours the *Dutch* do, even in our own Country: For in most Commodities the Earth brings forth, the Stock imployed in Planting and Managing of them, makes a great (in many the greatest) part of their Price; and consequently their Stock with them being rated at six in the Hundred, they may with great Gain under-sell us, our Stock with us being rated at ten.

And as they may out-Trade us and under-sell us, so are all Contributions to the War, works of Piety and Glory of the State, cheaper to them than to us, for the Use for Money going with us near double the rate it doth in other Countries, the giving the same Sum must needs be double the charge to us it is to them.

Amongst other things which the King, with

with ſo much Wiſdom delivered to the Houſe of Parliament, he committed to their Conſideration the Ballanceing of Trade and Commerce, wherein there is nothing of greater Conſequence, than the rate of Uſury, which holds no proportion with us and other Nations, to our diſadvantage, as by Experience we ſee and feel.

Neither is the high rate of Uſury leſs hurtful to Commerce within the Land, the Gain by Uſury being ſo eaſie, certain, and extream great, as they are not only Merchants and Trades-men, but Land-men, Farmers, and Men of Profeſſion that grow lazy in their Profeſſions, and become Uſurers; for the rate of Uſury is the Meaſure by which all Men Trade, Purchaſe, Build, Plant, or any other ways bargain.

It hath been the Wiſdom and Care of former *Parliaments* to provide for the preſervation of Wood and Timber; for which there is nothing more available than the calling down of the high rate of Uſury; for as the rate of Money now goeth, no Man can let his Timber ſtand, nor his Wood grow to ſuch Years growth as is beſt for the Common Wealth, but it will be very loſsful to him; The Stock of the Woods after they are worth forty or fifty Shillings the Acre, growing faſter at ten in the Hundred, than the Woods themſelves do.

And

And for *Shipping*, which is the ſtrength and ſafety of this Land; I have heard divers Merchants of good Credit ſay, that if they would Build a Ship, and let it to any other to employ, they cannot make of their Money that way counting all charges, tear and wear, above ten or twelve in the hundred, which can be no gainful Trade, Money it ſelf going at ten in the Hundred.

But in the *Low-Countries*, where Money goeth at ſix, the Building of Ships, and Hiring them to others, is a gainful *Trade*; and ſo the Stock of Rich Men, and the Induſtry of Beginners are well joyned for the Publick.

And yet that which is above all the reſt, the greateſt Sin againſt the Land is, that it makes the Land it ſelf of ſmall value, nearer the Rate of new found Lands, than of any other Country, where Laws, Government, and Peace have ſo long Flouriſhed; for the high Rate of Uſury makes Land ſell ſo cheap; and the cheap Sale of Land is the cauſe Men ſeek no more by Induſtry and Coſt to improve them.

And this is plain, both by Example and Demonſtration: For we ſee in other Countries, where the Uſe of Money is of a low Rate, Lands are generally ſold for thirty, forty, and ſome for fifty Years Purchaſe.

And we know, by the Rule of Bargaining, that if the Rate of Uſe were not greater here than in other Countries; Lands were then as good a penny worth at twenty Years Purchaſe, as they are now at ſixteen: For Lands being the beſt Aſſurance, and ſecureſt Inheritance, will ſtill bear a Rate above Money.

Now if Lands were at thirty Years Purchaſe, or near it, there were no ſo cheap Purchaſe as the amendment of our own Lands; for it would be much cheaper to make one Acre of Land, now worth five Shillings by the Year, to be worth ten Shillings, or being worth ten to be worth twenty Shillings, and ſo in *Proportion*; than to purchaſe another *Acre* worth five or ten *Shillings*.

And in every Acre thus Purchaſed to the owner, by the amendment of his own, there were another Purchaſed to the Common-Wealth.

And it is the Bleſſing of God to this Land, that there are few places of it to which he hath not given means, by reaſonable Coſt and Induſtry, greatly to amend it, in many to double the value, ſo as in time, if, for their own good, Mens Induſtry were compelled that way, the Riches and Commodities of this Land will near be doubled.

Then would all the wet Lands in this

Kingdom

Kingdom soon be drained, the barren Lands mended by Marle, Sleech, Lime, Chalk, Sea-sand, and other means, which, for their profit, Mens Industry would find out.

We see with how great Industry and Charge our Neighbours, the *Dutch*, do drain and maintain their Lands against the Sea, which floweth higher above them, than it doth above the lowest parts of our drown'd Lands.

I will admit a great deal to their Industry, but I should very unwillingly grant, that they are so much more ingenious and industrious than we, as that all the odds were therein.

Certainly, the main cause of it is, that with us Money is dear, and Land cheap; with them Land is dear, and Money cheap; and consequently the Improvement of their Lands at so great a charge with them, is gainful to the Owners, which with us would be lossful; for Usury going at ten in the hundred, if a Man borrow five Pounds, and bestow it on an Acre of Ground, the amendment stands him in ten Shillings the Year, and being amended, the Land is not worth above fifteen Years Purchase.

But if the Use of Money went at no more with us, than in other places, then five Pound bestowed upon an Acre of Ground, would stand

ſtand a Man but in 5 or 6 Shillings a Year, and the Acre of Land ſo amended would be worth, as hath been ſhewed, ſix and twenty or thirty Years Purchaſe.

Whereby it appeareth, that as the Rate of Uſe now goeth, no Man (but where the Land lieth extraordinarily happily for it) can amend his Land, but to his own loſs; whereas if Money were let as it is in other Countries, he might beſtow more than double ſo much as now he may, and yet be a great gainer thereby; and conſequently, as was before remembred, ſhould to his own benefit Purchaſe Land to the Common-wealth.

Neither would ſuch Purchaſe of Land to the Common-wealth, be the benefit to the Landed Men only, the benefit would be as much to the poor *Labourers* of the Land; for now when *Corn* and other *Fruits* of the Land, which grow by Labour, are cheap, the *Plough* and *Matlock* are caſt into the Hedge, there is little work for poor Men, and that at a low Rate; whereas, if the mendment of their own Lands were the cheapeſt Purchaſe to the Owners, if there were many more People than there are, they ſhould more readily be ſet at work, at better Rates than they now are, and none that had their Health and Limbs could be Poor, but by their Extreameſt Lazineſs.

And as the high Rate of Usury doth imbase Lands, so it is as great a hindrance to *Discoveries*, *Plantations*, and all good Undertakings, making it near double as chargeable to the Adventurers (Money being at ten in the hundred) as it is in other *Countries*, where the Use of Money is so much lower.

Now let us see the contrary, and conceive if Usury were tollerated at fifteen or twenty in the hundred (and I fear many Borrowers, all things considered, pay above ten) what the condition of things would then be; and if it appear how *desperate* the hurt would be which that would bring; it may (at least upon good reason) perswade us how great the good would be of calling it down.

Certainly, it must of necessity come to pass, that all Trades would in a short time decay: For few or none (and reckon the hazard at nothing) yield so great a gain as twenty in the hundred; and all other *Nations* might with so great gain out-trade and under-sell us, that more than the *Earth* would of her self bring forth, we should scarce raise any thing from it, even for our own use within the Land; and Land might be so much imbased, as men might afford without loss to themselves, to carry the *Compost* out of their *Closes*, upon their next adjoyning Lands to mend them: So far should we be from *Marling*, *Li-*

ming, *Draining*, *Planting*, and any other *Works* of *Cost* or *Industry*, by which Lands are purchased to the Common-Wealth. So far from Building, making of Havens, Discoveries, new Plantations, or any other Actions of Vertue and Glory to the State; for private Gain is the Compass Men generally Sail by.

And since we cannot, without extraordinary diligence, Plant, Build, Drain, or any other way amend our Lands, but it will be dearer to us, than the Purchase of others, Money being at ten in the hundred; if Money then should go at twenty in the hundred, the charge of mending our Land would be doubled, and the Land abated to seven or eight Years Purchase; and consequently all Works of Industry and Charge, for improving of Lands, would be quite neglected and given over: We should only eat upon one another with Usury, have our Commodities from other Nations, let the Land grow barren and unmanured, and the whole State in short time come to Beggary.

Against this (perhaps) may be objected, *That before the* 37 *of* H. 8. *there was no limitation of Usury, and how did we then?*

To this may be answered, That in those times there was a stricter Band in that Point upon Mens *Consciences*: So far forth as Usurers were in the same case as Excommunicate Persons

Persons, they could make no Wills, nor were allowed Christian Burial.

Therefore let us, for our *Fore-fathers* sake, hope, that the tye upon their Consciences then, was a greater restraint of Usury, than the Statute of ten in the hundred is now: I fear Fornication is too frequent amongst us; yet, thanks be to God, not so much used as where there is allowance of Curtizans and Stews.

The *Objections* likely to be made against the calling down of Money; are,

First, *That general Objection of Ignorance against all Changes, be they never so necessary and apparently good, that it hath been so a long time, and been well enough; what will become of the alteration we cannot tell; why then should we make any change?*

Secondly, *That as in Bodies Natural, so in politick, great and sudden Changes are most commonly dangerous.*

Thirdly, *That Money will be suddenly called in, and so all Borrowers greatly Prejudiced.*

Fourthly, *That Money will be harder to come by, and thereby Commerce greatly hindred.*

Lastly, *That much Money of Foreigners, by reason of the high Rate of Usury, is brought over here to be managed at Interest, which would be carried away again, if the rate of Usury should be called down.*

To the First.

That Money hath long gone at Ten, and things been well enough.

It is answered, That it is not long that the practice of *Usury* hath been so generally used, without any sense or scruple of the unlawfulness of it; for Mens *Consciences* were hardened to it with example and custom, by degrees, and not upon the sudden.

And as the beginning of many dangerous Diseases in Healthful Bodies, so the beginning of many Inconveniences in a State, are not presently felt.

With us, after that with long Civil-Wars the Land was half unpeopled; so, as till of late Years, it came not to his full stock of People again, there being the same quantity of Land to half the number of People; the surplusage of our In-land Commodities must needs be so great, that, tho' Trade were not equally Ballanced with us and other Nations, we could not but grow Rich.

Besides, *France* and the *Low-Countries* were for many Years half laid waste with *Wars*, and so did trade but little, nor manage their own *Lands* to their best advantage; whereby they did not only not take the Trade and Market from us, which now they do, but they themselves were fed and cloathed by us, took our Commodities from us at great high Rates.

Whereas

Whereas now we see the *Dutch* do every where out-trade us, and the *French* feed us with their Corn, even in Plentiful Years.

So as now our *Land* being full stock'd with *People*, our Neighbours industrious and subtile in Trade, if we do not more equally Ballance Trade, and bring to pass that we may afford the Fruits of our Land, as cheap as other *Countries* afford the same of the same kind; we must (tho' we leave a number of our *Superfluities*, as *God* forbid but we should) in a short time grow Poor and Beggarly.

And in this condition ten in the hundred, in a little more time, will as well serve to do it, as if Money were at twenty: For (as was before remembred) in most of the Commodities the Earth bringeth forth, the Stock employed in Planting and Managing of them, makes a great part of their Price; and consequently, they may, with great gain to themselves, under-sell us; our Stock with us going at double the rate that theirs goes with them.

This we see and feel too well by the Experience at this present; for having a great Surplusage of *Corn*, we can find no vend for it; the *French* with their own, the *Dutch* with the Corn of *Poland*, every where supplying the Markets at cheaper Rates than we can afford it.

And even our *Cloaths*, which have hitherto been the Golden Mine in *England*, I have heard many Merchants ſay, That (except it be in ſome few of the fineſt ſort of them, which is a Riches peculiar to this Nation) other *Countries* begin to make them of their own Wool, and, by affording them cheaper than we may, ſo to take our Markets from us.

And this I hope may in part ſerve for Anſwer to the next Objection; that all great and ſudden *changes* are commonly *dangerous*; for that *Rule* holds true, where the Body Natural or Politick is in perfect ſtate of Health, but where there is a declining (as I have ſome cauſe to fear there is, or may ſoon be with us) there to make no alteration is a certain way to Ruin.

To the Third.

That Money will ſuddenly be called in, and ſo all Borrowers greatly Prejudiced.

For that there may be a clauſe in the end of the Statute whenſoever it ſhall be made: That it ſhall be lawful for all that have lent Money at ten in the hundred, which is now forborn, & owing, to take for ſuch Money ſo lent and owing, during two Years after this *Seſſion* of *Parliament*, ſuch uſe as they might have done if this Act had not been made: Whereby *Borrowers* ſhall be in leſs danger of ſudden calling in of their Money, than now they

they are; for where the Lenders, upon Continuance of their old Security, may take ten in the hundred; upon new Security they may be content with less; so the calling in of their Money will be to their own Prejudice.

And if there be any Borrower to whom this giveth not sufficient Satisfaction, if such *Borrower* have *Lands* of value to pay his debts, the worst condition he can fear, is to have at the least twenty Years Purchase for his Land, wherewith to clear his Debts; for, as I said before, Land being the best Security, and securest Inheritance, will still bear a Rate above Money.

And so there being no Use allowed for Money above the Rate tollerated in other Countries, Land will as readily sell at twenty Years Purchase, as it doth now at twelve. And I think there is no Borrower that hath Land of value to pay his Debts, doth doubt if he will now sell his Land at ten Years Purchase, he might soon be out of Debt.

To the Fourth Objection.

That Money will be hard to be borrowed, and so Commerce hindred.

I answer, That it were true, if the high Rate of Usury did increase Money within this Land; but the high Rate of Usury doth enrich only the Usurer, and impoverish the Kingdom, as hath been shewed; and it is the plenty of Money within the Land that maketh Money easier to be borrowed, as we see by the Example of other *Countries*, where Money is easier to be borrowed than it is with us, and yet the Rate tollerated for Use is little more than half so much.

It is the high Rate of Use that undoeth so many of the Gentry of the Land, which maketh the number of borrowers so great; and the number of Borrowers must of necessity make Money the harder to be borrowed, whereas if Use for Money were at a lower Rate, Land, as hath been shewed, would be much quicker to be sold, and at dearer Rates, and so the Nobility and Gentry would soon be out of Debt, and consequently the fewer Borrowrrs, and so to Trades-men aud Merchants Money easie to be had.

Further, let us consider if Money were called down, what Usurers would do with their Money; they would not I suppose long be sullen, and keep it a dead stock by them; for that were not so much as the safest way of keeping it: They must then either imploy it in Trade, purchase Land, or lend for Use at such Rate as the Law will tollerate: If it quicken Trade, that is the thing to be desired, for that will enrich the Kingdom, and so make money Plentiful.

And yet need not any Borrower fear that Money will be so imployed in Trade, as that there will not be sufficient of Money to Pur-

chase

chase Land; where the *Purchaser* may have as much, or near so much, *Rent* by the Purchase of Land, as he can by putting his Money to Use; For a great number of Gentlemen and others in the Country, know not how to imploy any stock in Trade, but with great uncertainty, and less satisfaction to themselves, than the letting of their Money at a lower Rate, or Purchasing Land at twenty Years Purchase or upwards.

No doubt for the Present there would be great buying and selling of Land, till Men had cleared themselves, and payed their Debts: But in short time Land, as it is shewed before, would sell at so dear a rate, as Money let at a lower rate of use, would bring in proportion as great a rate above the Rent that would be made then by the Purchase of Land, as the rate of Money now is above the Rent of Land, Purchased at fourteen or fifteen Years Purchase, and so by consequence Money would then as easily be borrowed as it is now; and so much easier, as it would be more plentiful, and fewer Borrowers.

To the last and weakest Objections.

That there is now much Money of Foreigners *in the Land, to be managed at ten in the Hundred, which, if Money should be called down, would be carried out of the Land.*

There is no doubt it is true: But I desire to know, whether any Man think it better for the

the State, that they should now carry out one hundred Pounds, or seven Years hence two; or fourteen Years hence four; or one and twenty Years hence eight: For so in effect upon the Multiplying of Interest they do.

It will seem incredible to such as have not considered it, but to any that will but cast it up, it is plainly manifest, that a hundred Pounds, managed at ten in the hundred, in seventy Years, multiplies it self to a hundred thousand Pounds. So if there should be a hundred thousand Pounds of Foreigners Money now managed here at ten in the hundred (and that doth seem no great matter) that one hundred thousand Pound in threescore and ten Years, which is but the Age of a Man, would carry out ten Millions, which I believe is more than all the Coin at this present in the Land.

I know we cannot conceive how any such sum should be managed at Interest, yet this is sufficient to make us little to joy in Foreigners Money.

Besides, we must not conceive that the Money of Foreigners, which is here managed at Usury, is brought into the Land in ready Coin or Bullion: The Course is, That Merchants send over Bills of Exchange to their Factors, for which they receive our Money here; and this is the Money they manage at Interest, and so they eat us out with our own Money.

The

The old Comparison, which compares Usury to the Butlers Box, deserves to be remembred; whilst Men are at play, they feel not what they give to the Box; but at the end of *Christmass* it makes all, or near all, Gamesters loosers: And I fear the Comparison hold thus much farther, That there is as few escape that continue in Usury, as that continue Gamesters; a Man may play once or twice, and leave a Winner, but the use of it is seldom without Ruin.

Now because I know Mens private Interests doth many times blind their Judgments, and lest any should be tempted for their own, against the publick good; I will desire them to remember, that if they have Lands as well as Money, that what they lose in their Money, they shall get in their Land; for Land and Money are ever in Ballance one against the other; and where Money is dear, Land is cheap; and where Money is cheap, Land is dear.

And if there be any yet so hearty a well-wisher to ten in the hundred, as that he still thinks it fit to be continued, my wish is, That he and his Posterity may have the priviledge to borrow, but not to lend at that Rate.

In the beginning of this Treatise I did disclaim the Proofs of the unlawfulness of Usury, leaving them to Divines; this one only

only rising from the Premisses) which may serve for all, I think fit to set down :

It is agreed by all the Divines that ever were, without exception of any; yea, and by the Usurers themselves, That biting Usury is unlawful: Now since it hath been proved, that ten in the hundred doth bite the Landed Men, doth bite the Poor, doth bite Trade, doth bite the King in his Customs, doth bite the Fruits of the Land, and most of all the Land it self; doth bite all works of Piety, of Vertue and Glory to the State; no Man can deny but ten in the hundred is absolutely unlawful, howsoever happily a lesser Rate may be otherwise.

To the King, increase of his Customs.

To the Kingdom, increase of Land, by Enriching of this.

To the Nobility and Gentry, deliverance from Bondage and Debt.

To Merchants, continuance and flowrishing in their Trade.

To young Beginners in Trade and Commerce, the Fruits of their own Labours.

To Labourers, quick imployment.

To Usurers, Land for the Money.

Postscript.

SInce the foregoing Papers were delivered to the Press, Mr. *Henry Dakers* Merchant sent me a most rational and admirable Treatise concerning Trade, called, ENGLAND's INTEREST AND IMPROVEMENT, writ by *Samuel Fortrey*, Esq; *one of the Gentlemen of his Majesties Privy Chamber*, in which he mentions something concerning the Interest of Money, in the following Words, Page 42. *viz.*

In the last place, concerning the Use of Money; which being the Life and Sinews of Trade, it hath been the Opinion of some, that the greater Use were allowed for Money, the more would be the Profit of the Publick; for that Strangers finding a greater Benefit to be made of their Money here, than other where, would send it hither, whereby Money would be much more plentiful amongst us.

Indeed I should be of their opinion, if as soon as by this means great sums of Money were transported hither, all their Money should be confiscat to the Publick: But if otherwise, sure it cannot be denied, but the greater the Use, the more the profit to the Usurer, and loss to the Debtor, so as in a

few

few Years we should find our selves so little enriched thereby, that when the Principal should be again recalled, we should find but little Money left; all our own being wasted in Use. Wherefore indeed the true Benefit to the Publick, is, To set the Use of Money as low, or rather lower than in our Neighbour Countries it is; for then they would make no Profit out of us by that means, but rather we on them. And it is the clear Profit that we get of our own, that will make this Nation Rich, and not the great sums we are indebted to others.

Which I have here inserted, for such like Reasons:

First, That the World may see I am not singular in this Opinion, although I thought I had been so, when first I wrote the aforesaid *Observations*.

Secondly, For Confirmation of the Truth, by the Authority of a Person of such known Abilities.

Thirdly, To give the Author his due Honour of being the first Observer, *&c.*

And I am sorry I know not the ingenious Author of the former Tract, that I might do right to his Memory, *Who hath done more for his Country than would have been the Gift of some Millions of Pounds Sterling into the Publick Exchequer.*

www.ingramcontent.com/pod-product-compliance
Lightning Source LLC
Chambersburg PA
CBHW030618030726
47497CB00006B/1547
9783337348090